LAO

FOLK
TALES

LAOIS
FOLK
TALES

NUALA HAYES

ILLUSTRATED BY RITA DUFFY

The
History
Press
Ireland

This work is dedicated to the people of Laois

First published 2015

The History Press Ireland
50 City Quay
Dublin 2
Ireland
www.thehistorypress.ie

British Library Cataloguing in Publication Data.
A catalogue record for this book is available from the British Library.

ISBN 978 1 84588 866 4

Typesetting and origination by The History Press
Printed and bound by TJ International Ltd, Padstow, Cornwall

CONTENTS

Introduction and Acknowledgements

'Sometimes folklore cuts straight to the heart of life.
It illuminates history like a small pure flame
burning in the darkest corner of memory.'

Vincent Woods, writer and broadcaster[1]

I learnt about Laois mainly through the stories and lore that were shared with me when I had the good fortune to be appointed artist-in-residence with Laois County Council Arts Office in 2002.

My brief was to 'unearth' the oral stories in this midland county, which, up to that point, were relatively unknown to me. To those who live on the peripheries of the island, the Midlands are places you pass through to get to the other side. The mid-point, the centre where roads meet, is also a place of movement and action, and a historically strategic place to possess, if the aim was to conquer. I discovered in County Laois that the stories that are told are intrinsically bound up with the land-scape, the place and the history. The stories of ghosts and spirits are stories from the subconscious underworld, beyond the seen world. Many of the storytellers I met call themselves historians, yet they fully understand the purpose and value of the told story as a way of knowing the world and their place in it.

Henry Glassie makes the point in *Irish Folk History* that the local historians 'connect to an ancient and vital Irish idea by ordering history more in space than in time'.

By the end of my time in County Laois – almost two years and many stories later – I had collected and recorded nine CDs of oral stories and history from many parts of the county. These recordings are now part of the Laois Oral Archive Collection and are available to the public through the Library Service. Some of those people who so generously shared their stories are no longer with us, but their voices remain. The recorded material was also the basis for a six-part radio series called *Tales at the Crossroads*, which was produced in 2004 for RTÉ Radio One.

Thanks to the encouragement of Muireann Ní Chonaill, the Arts Officer, and with support from the Heritage Office, I also produced a video of the same name which was filmed by local artist Ray Murphy and edited by Sé Merry Doyle of Loopline Films.

A story told is never the same twice. The written word pins the story down and forces it into the straitjacket of sentences and grammar. And the written text cannot always capture the music of the voice, the pauses, the emphasis to make a point, or even a joke. Or can it? In retelling these stories in written form, I have tried to retain the voice of the person who told me the story. As a teller of stories myself, I found it difficult to write them down, but I resisted the temptation to change or 'improve' them. To 'tell' a story is to live in the moment along with a listener. To read a 'told' story is a very different experience. A story asks to be told aloud.

The much-repeated phrase at the end of a story also applies here: *Má tá bréag ann bíodh, ní mise a chum é* (If there is a lie in here, don't blame me – I didn't invent it!).

However, this time around, I had access to the riches of the National Folklore Collection at UCD, to the local libraries in Stradbally and in Portlaoise, and to the published work of people such as Laois archaeologist Helen M. Roe, who collected *Tales, Customs and Beliefs from Co. Laoghis* in 1939; John Canon O'Hanlon, who wrote the mammoth work *A History of the Queen's County*, as well as collections of folk tales and local legends, which were published under his pseudonym, Lageniensis. Brother Dan Hassett FSC of the De la Salle Order in Castletown also collected and collated local lore and stories in 1985.

The collection of John Keegan's *Selected Works*, edited by Tony Delaney, is always a rich source of stories and poems from his short lifetime (1816–1849). A *History of Stradbally Co. Laois*, compiled by the Stradbally Historical Project in 1989, was also very useful.

However, the real pleasure in the process of compiling this work was meeting the very generous people who shared their time and their stories with me first, in 2002 and now thirteen years later in 2015.

Grateful thanks to Paddy Heaney, Paddy Dooley, Mick Dowling, Michael Clear, Dan Culleton, Johanna O'Dooley, Adrian Cosby, John F. Headen, Roghan Headen, Arthur Kerr, Hugh Sheppard, Paddy Laffin, Tina Mulhall, Seán Murray of Laois Archaeology, Hugh O'Rourke, Jimmy Fitzpatrick, the past pupils of Camross National School and the families of the late Jenny McGlynn and Frank Fogarty, for allowing me to reproduce their stories.

I am grateful to the management and members of Laois County Council; to Arts Officer Muireann Ní Chonaill, and the staff at the Arts Office, to Heritage Officer Catherine Casey and to Bernie Foran, County Librarian, for their support and enthusiasm for the project. It was a great boon to stay at the Arthouse in Stradbally, so close to the beautiful hills and lush valleys, which feature in many of the stories.

Julie Shead, librarian at Stradbally Library, thank you.

Míle buíochas to Criostóir Mac Cárthaigh of An Roinn Béaloideasa/Department of Folklore at UCD for his help sourcing material and to storyteller Aideen McBride, without whose encouragement I might never have begun. Thanks also to my friend and colleague, Jack Lynch for perusing the manuscript with a beady eye.

I am delighted to collaborate once more with Rita Duffy, who provided such vibrant images to illustrate the stories. Folklore and story is a rich source of inspiration to her as an artist, and her enthusiasm and energy keeps me spinning on. Thanks also to the photographer Stanislav Nikolov who documented all the drawings.

Nuala Hayes, 2015

Rock of Dunamase, County Laois.

1

THE ORIGIN
STORY OF LAOIS

The mythical origins of the Laoighsigh, the people of Laois, tells us that they were descended from the great Conall Cearnach, renowned among the Red Branch Knights and leader of the army of Conor Mac Neasa, King of Ulster, whose headquarters was at Emain Macha, now known as Navan Fort, in County Armagh.

It was said that Conall Cearnach fought against Queen Maedhbh of Connacht for seven years. After his defeat at the Battle of Ros na Rí alongside the River Boyne, he came south. The Book of Leinster tells us that he had two sons, Iriel Glúnmhar and Lughaidh Laoiseach Ceann Mór (Laoiseach of the Big Head). Laoiseach Ceann Mór was the one to watch.

Around the year AD 112, the King of Leinster looked for assistance against an invasion from Munster and our man Laoiseach was successful in defeating the Munstermen at Mullaghmast, Coolrus and Magh Riada, and banished them finally at another battle at Móna Droichead near Borris-in-Ossory. As a reward for his brilliant leadership Laoiseach was given Dunamase and its surrounding territories. It is from this man that Laois got its name.

With the Fort at Dunamase as his centre, he divided the area under his control into seven. Better known as 'the seven tribes of Laois', a portion was given to each of his seven followers.

The O'Moores, Lughaidh Laoiseach's own descendants, are likely to have got their name from his big head, his *ceann mór*. The others were the O'Kellys, the O'Devoys, the O'Dorans, the O'Lalors, the O'Dowlings and the McEvoys. The leaders of these tribes were awarded many privileges at the court of the king, including the right to a sirloin of beef from a cow killed for the king's table. They acted as counsellors and treasurers as well as distributing the king's bounty to bards, musicians and other professionals. Rory O'Moore had a hand in setting up the Franciscan monastery in Stradbally and his family is praised in Leabhar na Nua Congbhaile, now known as the Book of Leinster.

The O'Moores and all these other family names are still prevalent in Laois and in the surrounding counties. In the main it was the ancestors of these septs or tribes that were the opposition to the invasions and plantations which make up the history of this part of the Midlands of Ireland. This is a place where the old roads crossed, where the story of Ireland was played out. The location, created by the boundary of the River Barrow to the north and east, the River Nore to the south and the Slieve Bloom Mountains to the west, with rich lands in the valleys in between, makes the county of Laois a beautiful place in which to live, as well as a place worth fighting over.

While searching for stories in Laois, I came across various spellings of the name which awakened my curiosity. In a handwritten book of stories collected in 1927 by Áine Uí Chiarbhaic of Ballyadams NS, she writes 'Stories from Laoghis' in the frontispiece. This book is in the National Folklore Collection.[2]

Then there is Leix, from which Abbeyleix, or *Mainistir na Laoise*, gets its name. From the sixteenth century, when the lands of Laois were annexed by the English Crown, the area was known as Queen's County, after Queen Mary.

The sister county, now Offaly, was called King's County. The principal fort or *dún*, which was up to then an O'Moore stronghold, was taken by the English forces and the town Maryborough developed after the fort was built. So it was until we achieved independence from England in 1921 and the decision to change the name was voted in by the Local County Council. Queen's County became County Laois and Maryborough became Portlaoise.

In between all the tussles for power, the battles and the conflicts, life went on, children were born and the people survived on the fruits of the good soil, the water from the many spring wells and the legends and stories, which nourish the imagination.

2

FIONN MACCUMHAILL AND THE SALMON OF KNOWLEDGE

When I first came to Laois in 2002, I wasn't aware that Fionn MacCumhaill, the legendary warrior of ancient times, was associated with the this part of Ireland. In fact I shouldn't have been surprised because, like all popular folk heroes, his reputation spread like wildfire and there are stories of the Fianna in many places. I discovered that Fionn's name is still remembered in Laois in the town of Ballyfin, Baile Fhionn, Fionn's home place. I visited fifth and sixth class in Camross National School and when I asked the young people if they had any stories, first up was the story of how Fionn gained wisdom, told to me by a twelve-year-old girl named Katy Wallace. She told it as an introduction to another story, which follows this one.

When Fionn was only a young lad, his father Cumhall was killed in a battle. Mórna, his mother, feared his father's enemies would come after him too, so she sent him to live in the Slieve Bloom Mountains where he would be reared by two wise women named Bodhmhall and Liath Luachra.

They taught him all the skills they knew. He learned how to fight, to hunt, to run as fast as a hare and faster than a hound. He could make his way through a thick forest without breaking a twig or making a sound. He learned to respect the creatures of earth, river and sky and only to hunt when he needed to eat.

However the women were not skilled in poetry. In those days, poetry was a skill that only the druids, who spent years studying it, could master. So they sent him to live and work with an old druid, a poet named Finnegas, who lived alongside the River Boyne.

Finnegas taught him the language, the rhymes and the metres of poetry for an hour or two every day. The rest of the time, he spent fishing. He loved fishing and spent hours, days and years fishing for the salmon of knowledge. It was said that the first person to taste the flesh of this salmon would gain all the knowledge of the world. This particular salmon passed up the river every year to lay its eggs. Finnegas had spent years of his life studying but he realised he was not a master. He had never found the secret wisdom of the salmon. The wisdom of the legendary salmon of knowledge, which swam in the waters of the River Boyne, was all he desired.

After years of failure, Fionn was there with him at the moment of success. The young boy watched as he caught the speckled fish. He saw his joy and delight as he struggled to land the salmon.

Now, the truth was that Finnegas was skilled in many ways, but cooking a fish was not one of them, so he asked Fionn to help him. Fionn had been well taught by the women of the Slieve Bloom Mountains. He made a fire and began to cook the fish.

As he watched it cooking away on the spit over the fire, he noticed a blister appearing on the skin of the salmon. He pressed the blister to smooth the skin and in the process burnt his finger. He put his finger in his mouth to cool it and had the first taste of the salmon of knowledge. Finnegas came out to see how he was getting on. When he looked at Fionn, he recognised the knowing in his eyes.

'Did you taste the salmon?'

'I just pressed the blister on the skin,' Fionn replied, 'so it would be perfect for you.'

Finnegas spoke with the sadness of a man who knew that the gift of wisdom would never be his. 'I cannot teach you anymore. You already have all the knowledge in the world. Go on and be leader of the Fianna!'

And that he did, but that's another story!

3

FIONN AND
HIS SLIOTAR

Fionn loved to play hurling. One day he was out in his back garden, hitting his sliotar up in the air with his hurley. A bird flew by. This bird had lost one of the eggs from its nest and thought the ball was the missing egg, so it caught it in its beak as it flew through the air.

Fionn was devastated. He loved his hurley and his ball; they were his most treasured possessions, so he decided to go looking for the ball.

He lived in the Slieve Bloom Mountains so he looked all over the mountains, and in the trees that covered them, searching everywhere for the nest. He couldn't find it, so he decided to go to Offaly to look there. He went as far as the River Shannon. He crossed the river and searched all the counties around it, until he got to County Clare. There, up on the Cliffs of Moher, was a huge nest and inside was the bird, sitting on his hurling ball!

Fionn was very happy he had found the ball, but he didn't know what to do. How could he get his ball back without disturbing the bird? In the end, he decided he would go looking for the lost egg.

His mother was very worried by now. She called around to her friends in the Slieve Bloom Mountains, but no one knew where he was. Then she noticed the hurley and saw that the ball was missing. She guessed he was off somewhere looking for it.

Fionn searched throughout Munster for the egg, then he went up to Connacht and Ulster. Then back he came to the mountains of Laois and there, lying on a patch of grass, he found the egg. He was so glad it wasn't broken.

He went the whole way back to Clare with the egg. When he got a chance while the bird was away, he put the egg back in the nest.

The mother flew back. She looked at the sliotar and she looked at the egg and she knew which one of them was hers.

So Fionn got his hurling ball back. He went home and told his friends and his mother the story, but none of them believed him.

But he didn't really mind because he knew it was true![3]

4

The Birth
of Oisín

*The story of the birth of Oisín is one of my favourite stories.
I have told it for many years without realising that it has strong
connections with ancient districts in County Laois, Killeshin
and Sleatty. Killeshin was once Cill or Gleann Ossian, or Oisín,
in the Irish language. Sleatty is in Sliabh Mairghe, the Slieve
Margy Mountains, which overlook the huge plains of Leinster
across to the highest peaks of the Wicklow Mountains and
southwards towards Mount Leinster in County Wexford.*

*Fionn MacCumhaill himself, they say, was born in these
mountains and fostered by his aunt Bobal Bendrond,
the Druidess wife of Cucend of Teamhar Mairge.*

But enough of the background. Here's the story.

It was evening time. Fionn MacCumhaill and his two dogs, Bran
and Sceolán, were coming home, tired after a day's hunting in the
hills. Fionn walked slowly, enjoying the peace and quiet after the
excitement of the day. The two wolfhounds padded along beside
him. Suddenly a deer leapt from a bush and the dogs began to
bark. Fionn began to shout, urging the dogs on, 'Ar aghaidh leat, a
Bhran! Ar aghaidh leat, Sceolán!'

Soon they were chasing the deer through the smooth valley, all of them in steady, beautiful flight. Suddenly the deer stopped and lay on the ground with the calm of an animal without fear. But the dogs didn't stop. They continued to race towards her.

'They'll pull her apart,' Fionn thought to himself.

But the dogs didn't go in for the kill. When they reached the doe, they stopped and began to sniff and to play around her as though she was another dog – and an interesting one at that. Fionn was astonished. He had never seen the likes of it before and when he eventually caught up with his hounds, he put out his hand and the doe nuzzled her soft black nose into the upturned palm.

Without fear there is no hunt. Fionn decided that this was no ordinary deer. He decided to bring her back to his *dún* (fort) and protect her. She joined the herd that grazed the plains around the fort, where the Fianna were forbidden to hunt.

One day the door to Fionn's room opened and a beautiful young woman walked in. Fionn was surprised and asked who she was.

'My name is Sadhbh,' the woman replied, 'and I have come to ask for your protection. I am in terror of the Fear Dorcha.'

As soon as he heard this, Fionn realised that this was a woman of the other world and that she had come to him first in the form of a deer. 'He is everywhere,' she said. 'He looks up at me from the water and looks down at me from the sky. His voice commands and demands. I cannot escape and I am afraid!'

When she spoke the words, a deep desire to protect her stirred in Fionn's heart and he invited her to stay. She did and in no time at all they were inseparable. Fionn lost interest in everything, including hunting, fishing, feasting and *ficheall* (chess). Nothing interested him, apart from being with this beautiful woman, Sadhbh.

His mates in the Fianna were not impressed.

One day news came that the dreaded Lochlannaigh (the Danes) had rounded the Hill of Howth and were preparing to attack. At the best of times, Fionn had no time for these men from the north, with their long boats, their long legs and their long, wild hair, but this time they were coming between him and his beloved. He promised he would be back soon. He bade farewell to the love of his life and set off with his comrades to face the foe. The servants were left with orders to take good care of her while he was gone.

One day, not long after this, the sound of *an dord Fhiann*, the hunting horn used by the Fianna, was heard from the hill outside the fort.

When Sadhbh heard the sound she ran outside. A figure who was the image of Fionn, with two dogs just like Bran and Sceolán, stood on the crest of the hill. Sadhbh was overjoyed. Her husband had returned! And she had great news for him. She was expecting their child. The servants tried to stop her but she wouldn't be held back. Horrified, they watched as she ran up the hill. The tall man raised

The birth of Oisín

his hand to strike her with a holly bush. At that moment, Sadhbh disappeared, but in her place there appeared a doe, frightened and shivering and backing away in terror. Three times the creature tried to escape and three times the savage dogs followed her and pulled her back. When eventually the servants reached the spot, there was nothing to be seen. They could hear the sounds of dogs barking and the beat of feet running, but the sounds seemed to be coming from all directions, so it was impossible to follow them.

Having dispatched the invaders back to wherever they came from, and satisfied that any who remained in Ireland were well dead, Fionn returned to his *dún*.

He didn't wait for the victory celebrations. He headed straight home where he hoped that the love of his life would be waiting to meet him, her arms outstretched in greeting.

The sight that greeted him when he returned was far from what he had imagined. There were few people around and those who were avoided his eyes. What had happened? He caught the eye of *Garbh Crónán,* the Rough Buzz, the man whose job it was to see to the opening and closing of the gates.

'*Cad a tharla*?' Fionna asked. 'What happened?'

When the story was told to him, Fionn dropped his head in despair and went back to his room. He stayed there, alone, for many weeks. When eventually he did emerge, he trained five special dogs for hunting. He wanted to be sure that if a deer were caught and it happened to be Sadhbh, she would not be killed. One day he was out again hunting with his men when they heard the sound of a dog fight in the distance. They followed the sound and found the five special dogs in a circle, holding off the rest of the snarling, growling pack.

A small fair-haired boy, no more than 3 years of age, stood calmly in the centre of the circle, looking around without fear. Fionn called the dogs off and went towards the boy. The boy didn't speak a language he understood, but something in his look, his alert and calm eye, reminded him of a doe. Fionn took the boy home and began to speak to him and teach him and, when he was old enough, to ask him questions.

A young child doesn't remember the past very well, but the boy did remember living alone in a cave with a deer he loved. There was always food left at the mouth of the cave and sometimes a dark figure would cast a shadow and the deer would disappear.

Fionn called the boy Oisín, which means 'young deer'. He was raised on the mountains of Slieve Mairge by Fionn's own foster mother. He learnt all the skills of the Fianna and he grew up to be a warrior and a poet. He came to be known as the last of the Fianna.

But that, as they say, is another story.

5

FIONN MACCUMHAILL AND THE HOUSE OF DEATH

Fionn learned the skills of hunting from the women in the Slieve Bloom Mountains, so it was no wonder that it was there he often went to hunt many years later, when he eventually became the leader of the Fianna, that legendary band of warriors. The Fianna were as famous as footballers, golfers, or celebrity rock stars are now. They had the run of the country and were welcomed everywhere.

One time Fionn was hunting in the mountains with his companions, Conán Maol Mac Mórna, Diarmuid O'Duibhne, his own son Oisín and his grandson Oscar. They stayed out too late and when evening came, they had no shelter for the night. They walked on for a while, then Fionn saw a house in the distance. By the light which shone in the window, they could see that it was inhabited. They went up to it and banged at the door. The door was opened by an ancient old man with a long, white beard.

'Fionn MacCumhaill, you're welcome,' he said. 'Come in, all of you.'

'You know us?' Fionn asked.

'Indeed I do,' said the man. 'Who doesn't know the stories of Fionn and the Fianna, and all about your skills and your courage? You are more than welcome. Come in, for sure, you can rest and eat here.'

In they went. The room was comfortable enough. A fire was burning and a big wooden table in the middle of the room, laid

out with delicious food, was all set up for eating. In the corner of
the room there was a lamb tethered to the wall. Sitting by the fire
sat the most gorgeous-looking girl they had ever seen. Her beauty
alone would light up a house. A black cat sat by her feet.

'Sit and be comfortable,' said the man. 'You'll have something
to eat?'

'We will indeed and thank you,' said Fionn and the others
nodded. They couldn't take their eyes away from the young
woman. The old man nodded at the girl and told her to get the
food ready.

Just then the lamb broke away from his tether and leapt up on the
table, causing consternation.

Oscar was the first to move. He would impress the young woman.
He leapt on to the table and caught the lamb, but the lamb was
stronger than he looked. It shoved him away and he landed on
his backside. Oisín, Oscar's father, had a go, but the lamb kicked
out at him, tossed him over and he landed head over heels. Then
Diarmuid was headbutted and thrown to the ground. Conán Maol
Mac Mórna, a huge lump of a man, was a bit slow on the uptake,
but he was a great fighter. But when he approached the lamb, he was
also thrown across the room. Now, thought Fionn, I suppose I'm
the next to go. He grabbed at the lamb, but it was as steady as a
rock. One little nudge and Fionn, the great warrior, landed flat on
his back and couldn't move a muscle.

'That's some lamb you have there,' he said to the man. Then
the cat, who was sitting by the fire, came over and lifted the tether
from around the neck of the lamb. The lamb followed it meekly
back to its place in the corner. This caused some astonishment but
the lads said not a word. It was all very strange.

Then when the food was ready, they sat down to eat and enjoy it.

Afterwards the old man showed them the room they would all
sleep in for the night. There were plenty of beds there. They weren't
long settling in when the door opened and the girl they had all
been admiring walked in carrying a candle and went over to a
small bed by the window. She got in under the blanket and blew
out the candle.

None of the men in the room could get a wink of sleep, but they pretended they did. When the odd snore could be heard and Oscar, the youngest, thought the rest of them were asleep, he got out of bed and quietly went over to the girl in the corner. She opened her eyes.

'Oscar,' she said, 'you had me once, but you thought little of me and you will never have me again.'

Oscar returned to his bed, disheartened. Then Oisín slipped over to her, and he too got the same response, as did Diarmuid and Conán Maol. They all returned like gentlemen to their beds, each wondering what she might have said to the others. Fionn, who was still awake, was well aware of what was going on. But he was the leader and therefore, he assumed, very attractive to women. So he approached her, smiling. She looked at him and smiled back.

'Fionn,' she said, 'I once was yours, but you thought so little of me and I will never be yours again.'

Fionn had been with a lot of women and thought he remembered them all, but this beautiful woman, he didn't recognise at all.

The next morning, before they left the house, Fionn spoke to the old man.

'We are grateful for the hospitality,' he said, 'but this is a very strange house. What's going on here? That lamb was so strong, none of us could lift it, but the cat, who is much weaker, just carried it off as though it was as light as a feather.'

'Ah,' said the man. 'That lamb is Life. Life has its own will. And the cat – well, the cat is Death. Only Death can control Life.'

'And that young girl?' said Fionn. 'Who is she? She seems to have known us all. But I can't recognise her at all?'

'That girl is Youth. You all had her once, you know, and you were careless and thought little of her, and now you will never have her again.'

'And who are you?' Fionn asked.

'Ah,' said the old man. 'My name is Time and I hold power over Life, over Death and especially over Youth.'

6

FIONN AND THE LEIX GIANT

I've heard it said in Laois that there were no giants, only giants of men. If that's the case, it could be said that Fionn was one of them.

There is a large rath (a circular enclosure surrounded by a high ditch or wall), situated on a high hill overlooking Ballyadams and Ballintubbert. The Hill of Allen in County Kildare, where the Fianna had their fortress, is clearly visible from the Rath Mór. Fionn MacCumhaill hunted on these plains and was accustomed to spending the night resting in Rath Mór.

It was here he challenged the Leix giant to throw the great stones from the hill of Tullymoy.

One day, when Fionn MacCumhaill was on one of his hunting expeditions, he met a giant in Leix who was as big and as powerful as himself. He was up in Tullymoy, near Stradbally, when he met this ferocious fellow and he couldn't resist the challenge.

'I bet you twenty boars of great weight,' said Fionn, 'that I can throw this stone farther than you can.'

There were many large stones on the hill. The Leix giant succeeded in throwing the stone as far as Loughglass, only about a mile away.

Fionn succeeded in throwing his stone as far as his own *dún* on the Hill of Allen in County Kildare, twenty miles away.[4]

Tullymoy has an ancient standing stone, known locally as *An Liagáin*. It is said to have been erected over one of the kings of Munster. An inscription, *'Hy Mórdha'*, was once clearly visible on the *Gallán* stone. There was a rumour that there was a crock of gold beneath the stone, but no one ever attempted to dig it out. People are reluctant to meddle with these old sites and with good reason.[5]

There was once an old, disused graveyard in the area. A story was told that a farmer who lived nearby levelled the graves and took the sods and clay to use as top dressing in a field close by. After some time, they tilled the field and sowed potatoes in it. Those potatoes could never be eaten as they found bits of bone and teeth in the centre of each potato.[6]

7

THE THIRD GATE AT
ROSSNACREENA

Here is another story from Niamh Collier,
recorded in 2002 at Camross National School.

Once upon a time there was a priest down here in Camross called
Father O'Carroll. There was also a group of soldiers that people
called the Black and Tans. They were ruthless and it was said that

they would stop at nothing to get the treasures of the church, which were in the care of Fr O'Carroll. One day Fr O'Carroll was contacted by his good friend, Feidhlim O'Farrell. He told him that the Black and Tans were coming after him and advised him to go on the run.

So they set off on their horses with the treasures and rode all day through County Laois, looking for a place to hide. They eventually got to the Slieve Bloom Mountains. Suddenly Feidhlim had a good idea. He told Fr O'Carroll to get off the horse and take off the horse's shoes. Then he produced some nails and a hammer and told him to put them on again, backwards. This way they would confuse the soldiers who were following them. Having done this, they kept going until they came to the lane between Ros na Doe and Rossnacreena. At the third gate at Rossnacreena, Feidhlim O'Farrell looked back. He saw it was hopeless. He could see plainly that the Black and Tans were behind them. He told the priest to bury the treasure there at the third gate and run off into the mountains. He would hold them off. Fr O'Carroll buried the treasure right there in the ground and set off while Feidhlim tried to hold off the soldiers. But he was killed at the gate. It is said that the treasure was never found and is still buried there. The priest was never heard of again but it is said that an angel in the form of a White Lady was sent by God to guard the gate. Some people have seen her, but I never have.[7]

8

THE BANSHEE FROM THE MOUNTAINS

Stories about the banshee (*bean sí*) were very popular and often repeated by people I met in the Slieve Bloom Mountains. It was believed that she followed certain families. Members of these families would hear her cry when someone was about to die. Very few people had actually heard her crying, or seen her, but many had met someone who said they had.

One man told me that a neighbour had told him one night that he'd heard the banshee crying near a house where a man called Culleton was dying. 'But,' the man said, 'she got the wrong Culleton. That man is a Protestant.' Apparently the banshee only follows Catholic families!

Understandably, it was stories of the banshee that the children I met at Camross were most eager to relate

'Normally, back then you were not meant to go out after twelve o'clock, because that's when the spirits are roaming. So anyway, my grandad was coming back from work and he saw an old woman on the wall. Because, when you are going into my house, there is a lane you have to go through. She was on the wall, combing her hair and singing some words. So my grandad asked her, "What are you doing out during the night?" She said nothing and leapt up on the horse. The horse died that night with severe cuts all over his body. My grandad came back that night and he was very sick too. But he's fine now and he told me that story.'

Here's another one. One night a man was coming back from work. He was a '*spailpín*' (a casual labourer). It had taken him three hours to get the bull in. Finally he managed to get him in, so he headed home. It was a lovely night. The crickets were singing away. After a time, he heard something behind him. It sounded like the rattling of chains. He kept on walking, thinking, 'Oh God, I hope this ghost doesn't hurt me.' So he sped up, but then he heard footsteps behind him. He heard banging, like wood hitting a rock three times, then the rattling of the chain, going plank, plank, plank. 'So anyways,' he said to himself, 'I have to face up to this ghost or he'll keep following me and eventually kill me. So he turned around and there behind him was the bull!

Another boy offered this ghoulish version of the story of the banshee: 'My great grandad's neighbour was out threshing the hay one day and next thing, the dog ran up to the corner of the field, over the hill. He couldn't see his dog. When he went up there to get the dog back, there was a banshee eating the dog. He went back to the house to get the gun, and when he got the gun, the dog, the hay, the blood and the banshee had all gone! Two weeks later, his bull disappeared and soon afterwards his cattle disappeared. He never found them. He went hunting for the banshee and he eventually found her in the banshee hole. He found bones in the hole. And they say he died hunting the banshee!

And another one from one of the boys from Camross National School: 'When my grandfather was small, about fifty years ago, he had an uncle and an aunt who lived up in the mountains in Kinnitty. Their names were Pat and Mary. One day he was helping Pat on the farm. There was a cow calving further up the lane. He went up with Pat, but they forgot the salt, which they always used when a calf was born, so he went back to get the salt. On the way back he saw Mary outside and he put his hand on their shoulder and he said, "I'm going in to get the salt." When he went inside, Mary was in there and she was brushing her hair. He wondered how Mary could be outside and inside at the same time. He collected the salt and went up and told Pat, who said it could have been the banshee. When they were walking back, they heard something crying. He was so scared that he decided he'd never go back there again and he never did!'[8]

9

THE RED FAIRY OF GRANTSTOWN

The old woman or the red fairy – the 'cailleach' in the Irish language – appears in many of the stories in County Laois and the surrounding counties. She is a force to be reckoned with and is not always depicted kindly.

Grantstown Lake is a beautiful place and it's now very well known as a fishing lake. It is popular with visitors from England, Scotland and, of course, many parts of Ireland, who fish mainly for eel, perch and pike.

In springtime the lakeside explodes with daffodils, hyacinths and bluebells, as well as the waterlilies that bob on the water. There are birds of all species there, including swans, which appear every year in the spring. Their arrival is taken as a sign of good weather. The swans leave when winter comes. The area around Grantstown is very popular for hunting fowl but the local gamekeeper will give you short shrift if he catches you shooting pheasants or other wild game.

But it is said that there was a time when there was no lake there at all, when instead there was a lovely fertile valley with wild flowers, daisies, primroses and bluebells in abundance. In the middle of the valley was a beautiful spring well, gurgling up from the centre of the earth, which was so deep that people believed there was no bottom to it.

Overlooking the valley was a simple little cabin, where Moya Liath, or Grey Mary Slattery, lived with four little children: three little boys and a *girsha* (a little girl). They weren't her own children, but the children of her daughter, Rose, who was dead and buried with her husband in the churchyard of Bordal not far from the valley.

Summer came and there was nothing to eat. The potatoes had failed, the corn was blasted, the cattle had died of distemper and no food could be had in the valley for love nor money. Moya had tried everything to feed the children. She boiled nettles and weeds and grass and whatever else she could lay her hands on. But the children cried and whinged because they were starving. One evening in July, when the sun had sunk behind the mountain, Moya sat at the door, trying to comfort the children, wiping the tears from their eyes and the snot from their noses. '*Dá fhaide an oíche, tiocfaidh an lá …*' (However long the night is, the day will come). They had no idea what she was talking about.

As she spoke a shadow crossed the door. Moya looked up and she saw a strange-looking little woman in front of her. Crooked and wrinkled, with hair as grey as Moya's, she wore a crimson cloak and her hair was tied up with a blood-red scarf. Moya had never seen her like before.

'Good evening,' she said, as she walked into the cabin.

'*Bail ó Dhia ort*, the blessings of God on you,' Moya replied.

'Save your breath to cool your porridge. Keep your blessings. I never asked for them,' the little woman replied.

'I wish I had porridge,' said Moya. 'If I had, I would find breath to cool it and to say a prayer for the good of my neighbours too!'

'Are you a good neighbour?'

'I think I am,' said Moya.

'I've no pot to boil my supper. Will you lend me yours?' the woman asked.

'I will, with a heart and a half, for I've no supper to boil.'

'Thank you, Moya,' said the woman. She grabbed the pot, which was full of water from the well for the children to drink at night.

'Can I ask you where do you live? I've never seen you around these parts before.'

'No matter where I live,' said the woman. 'The pot will be back to you in the morning. I give you my word. Goodnight!' As she turned from the door, she turned around suddenly. 'And let none of you look after me! If ye do, I'm warning you, I'll smash this pot into smithereens.' With that, she disappeared from their sight.

Next morning, Moya was up early to forage for some edible greens for the children's breakfast. 'Oh, I forgot about the pot,' she said out loud. 'That old hag never brought it back.'

'You're a liar, Moya Liath!' came the voice of the old woman from behind the door.

Moya opened the door and there was the pot, full to the brim with steaming stirabout porridge. There was a big yellow lump of delicious-looking butter melting in the centre.

She called the children down and in no time at all they emptied the pot. By the end of the day, their smiles had returned.

That evening, as the sun went down, the little red woman came back and borrowed the pot, with the same warning: 'Don't be looking after me now!' Next day, the pot of beautiful porridge topped with more golden butter was glistening in the sun outside the door.

This went on, day after day, for a week, and by the end of it, there wasn't a better-fed or happier family of children in the whole of Ossory.

One evening, the strange little woman appeared as usual. This time she said, 'Moya Liath, after tomorrow night, I'll be troubling you no more, for my time here has come to an end. I have orders to move. But I thank you for your neighbourly generosity.'

'My generosity!' Moya cried. 'What will we do without yours? What will become of us now and the hunger and sickness raging all over the country?'

'*Dá fhaide an oiche, tiocfaidh an lá,*' said the old woman, as she swung the pot away again.

'She's a quare little woman,' thought Moya. 'Well, if she's leaving soon, I've nothing to lose.' She looked out the door, her eyes following the figure of the old woman. 'I'll see where she is going at least, if nothing else.'

You can just imagine Moya's surprise when she saw that the little woman headed straight for the well in the middle of the valley. She raised the wooden lid and got into it, pot and all!

'I knew it. I always suspected she was a fairy and I was right!' said Moya.

Next day was a bad one for Moya. Her mind raced all day. The fairy woman was to visit for the last time. What would she do without food for the children after that? Then, as quick as a flash, an idea came to her. 'Well,' she thought, 'I have nothing to lose, have I?'

The sun was setting when the little red woman appeared again. 'This is my last time asking for the pot,' she said. 'I know you won't refuse me.'

'Indeed I won't. But I've no water for the night for the children and I've nothing to carry it in only the pot. So sit down there by the fire and I'll hop out for a drop from the well. I'll be back before you know it!'

The Red Fairy

The little red woman sat by the fire and Moya hobbled over to the well with the pot. She lifted the lid and filled the pot with water. She fastened the wooden lid on top and made the sign of the cross over it.

'Now,' she said to herself, 'my guess is she won't be able to lift it. If she can't, I'll make her promise me a bag of gold as long as my arm and a bag of meal that would flatten an ass.'

'What's keeping you?' the old woman shouted from the house. 'Will you be there all night?'

'I'm coming,' said Moya. 'Just get me that basin from under the dresser to keep the water in.'

The old woman grabbed the pot and set off with it as usual. Moya watched from the door as she got to the well and stooped to lift the lid, then she heard her raise a cry loud enough to wake the dead in the graveyard!

'Moya Liath! What have you done?' she screeched 'Raise the lid and let me into the well or you'll rue the day you ever set eyes on the red fairy of Grantstown!'

'I will,' said Moya. 'I will, if you promise me enough oatmeal to last a year and enough gold to put me and my seven generations nine days' march before poverty!'

'Is that what you say?' shouted the old woman in a voice that would shake a mountain.

'It is indeed, *a chara mo chroí*!' said Moya.

'Well then,' said the fairy. 'If I can't get into the water, the water will come to me.' She plucked a white hair from under her red scarf, muttered some words over it, flung it into the air and gave a whistle which echoed over the valley and the grey ruins of the Fitzpatricks' castle.

At that instant a thundering, gurgling sound was heard from within the well and the water burst through the lid with a terrific crash, then flowed furiously and spread itself across the valley in no time. The red woman disappeared. Moya ran as fast as her legs could carry her. She grabbed the children and dragged them up the hill to a place of safety as the water rushed and filled the valley and covered the well and the house and everything she had.

Next morning, when Moya came back to look for her cabin, a wide expanse of water met her eyes and the lovely valley was covered from that day to this with the bright waters of Grantstown Lake.

But the red woman wasn't finished yet. Scarcely had the flooding stopped when a mighty whirlwind blew up and swept over the lake, sweeping away everything in its path, levelling houses, towers, cornfields and trees, all belonging to the Fitzpatricks and the O'Moores.

After a day and a night, the storms ceased and the skies cleared and the sun shone on the lake and showed it as clear and as silver as glass. Then the waters were found to be teeming with fish of various shapes and sizes, all edible and delicate to the taste. The people of the area fished them and ate them with relish.

The fairy tempest had also blown in flocks of fowl which appeared throughout the lands of Laois and Ossory; birds more beautiful than any that had been seen in the area before, with red, green, blue and gold plumage. They were so tame that they would sometimes fly in the doors of houses, ready to be plucked and eaten! Moya lived to a good age and her grandchildren, when they were grown, told this marvellous story to their children, who have passed it on to us.

The plague ended and hunger disappeared and the good lands of County Laois became well known for their wealth and abundance right up to the present day.

Eileen Ahern, who told me a version of this story, is originally from Newcastle West in County Limerick, but she lived for forty years beside Grantstown Lake, which is in the southern part of County Laois, near the parish of Aghaboe, in the region of old Ossory.[9]

The Great Famine was a traumatic time for the impoverished Irish people and, understandably, the scarcity of folklore from this time reflects this. This story is sometimes called 'The Fairy's Revenge' and is part of John Keegan's collection of stories.

10

THE BEWITCHED BUTTER

This story comes from John Keegan's story in
Fairy and Folk Tales of Ireland *by W.B. Yeats.*

There was once a wealthy farmer named Bryan Costigan who lived with his wife Judy in the vicinity of Aghaboe in County Laois. He kept an extensive dairy and a herd of milch cows, and each year made a considerable amount of money through the sale of his milk and butter. Brian's cows were the finest and most productive in the county and his milk and butter were the sweetest.

His prosperity increased year after year, until, all of sudden, he noticed that his cattle no longer looked as good as they once had and the milk they produced was now weak and scanty and so bitter that even the pigs refused to drink it. Their butter was equally bad and gave off such a stench that even the dogs walked away from it. Bryan looked for remedies from all the quacks and 'fairy women' in the country, but none of them could help him in any way.

Bryan Costigan and his family saw ruin staring them in the face. They couldn't sell the cattle as they looked so miserable and emaciated. It was impossible to sell them to a butcher or to eat the flesh themselves as it was foul and putrid.

The unfortunate man was completely bewildered. He couldn't sleep at night. By day he wandered moodily through the fields, amongst his stricken cattle, like a lost soul.

Bewitched Butter   Peter D▪▪ 2015

One lovely warm evening at the end of July, Bryan's wife, Judy was sitting at the door, spinning at her wheel. The rhythm of the work distracted her mind from gloomy and agitated thoughts.

Down the lane leading up to the door, she saw the figure of an old woman walking barefoot, dressed in a scarlet cloak, with a crutch in one hand and a walking stick in the other. The woman hobbled up the lane towards her. For some strange reason, Judy felt a lift in her heart when she saw her, and greeted her warmly.

'You're welcome here,' she said, 'whoever you are.'

'I thought I would be,' said the woman, with a grin, 'or I wouldn't be troubling you.'

Judy invited her in to take a seat by the fire, but she refused and squatted on the ground beside the spinning wheel. She was a strange-looking creature with her leathery, lined skin, her long grey hair, her white linen skullcap and her deep-set, blood-shot eyes. She peered around as though she could see into the very depths of the earth.

Judy watched her with a mixture of curiosity, awe and pleasure.

'Missus,' the woman said after a long pause. 'I'm parched with the heat of the day. Can you give me a drink?'

'I can offer you nothing except water. I'm sorry,' said Judy.

'Are you the owner of the cattle beyond?'

'I am', said Judy and told her of the *cruachás* they were in with the cattle.

The old woman was quiet for a while as she peered around the house.

'Have you any milk from those cows in the house?'

'I have.'

'Show me some of it.'

Judy filled a cup with the milk and handed it to the little woman, who smelled it, tasted it, and spat it out on the floor.

'Where is your husband? I must see him.'

Bryan was called for and the old woman challenged him. 'Why haven't you sought a cure for these cattle?'

'A cure? I've sought cures till my heart was broken and all in vain. They are getting worse every day.'

'What will you give me if I cure them for you?'

'Anything we have,' Judy and Bryan spoke with one voice.

'Will you give me a silver sixpence?'

'Is that all?'

They offered more.

'No,' said the old one. 'I'm no cheat and I wouldn't even take sixpence, but I can do nothing unless I handle some of your silver.'

The sixpence was given to her and she pulled out a black ribbon from under her cap.

'Go now,' she said. 'And the first cow you touch with the ribbon, turn her into the yard, but be sure not to touch any other, or speak a word until you return. Don't let the ribbon touch the ground, for if you do, it's all over.'

Bryan took the ribbon and returned later, driving a red cow before him.

The old woman began to mutter and hum a tune as she approached the cow, then she began pulling hairs from her tail. The chanting continued until she had extracted nine hairs. The cow was returned to the pasture and the old woman ordered that milk be got from every cow in the herd.

Judy went off and returned with a large pail filled with the weak and watery milk, tinged with blood and mixed with corrupt matter. The old woman poured it into a churn, then she told them to fasten the doors and windows, build up the fire and begin churning.

'Speak no word while you work and before the sun goes down, we'll find the villain who's robbing you.' She wasn't shy when it came to giving orders.

Bryan locked the doors and the windows and began the process of churning the milk. The old *cailleach* sat by the blazing fire and continued her wild chant as, one at a time, she slowly threw the hairs from the tail of the cow into the fire. She watched them sizzle, then burn and she waited.

Finally, a loud cry of distress was heard outside the house. The old woman continued her singing. Footsteps approached the door.

'Open the door quick', the old woman shouted.

Bryan opened the door and they rushed into the yard, but the cry disappeared down the boreen.

'Something's gone wrong. The charm didn't work.'

She looked down and saw a piece of an old horseshoe, nailed to the threshold.

'No wonder,' she said. 'I brought the person we're looking for to the door, but she couldn't come further because of that horseshoe. Take it away and we'll try our luck again.'

Bryan removed the horseshoe from the doorway and, following the old one's directions, he reddened it and then placed it under the churn.

Brian and Judy returned to the churning and the old woman to her incantations as she began to burn the last of the hairs. As she got to the ninth, her face contorted, her teeth gnashed and her hand trembled as she spat out the words of her spell.

Once again the cry was heard and a woman was seen approaching the house quickly.

'What do we do now?' said Bryan.

'Say nothing to her. Give her whatever she wants and leave the rest to me.'

Bryan opened the door and saw his neighbour standing there in a distressed condition. Her name was Rachel Higgins. She told him that one of her best cows was drowning in a pool of water. She beseeched him. She was all alone and needed someone to help her. Bryan went with her, rescued the cow and came back in when he had finished.

Judy was busy making the supper.

'I suspected the trouble came from Rachel Higgins,' he said. 'But I couldn't be sure. She has five or six cows but she sells more butter every year than any of the neighbours who have more and better cows.'

'She'll have to be caught and stopped, before your luck will return,' said the old woman. 'I'll tell you what to do and if you follow my instructions we'll find the proof before morning. Tonight, at the hour of twelve o'clock, go to the field where your cows are and bring with you a couple of fast dogs. Hide yourselves and if you see anything approach the cows, be they man or beast, set the dogs on them. But they must draw blood if we are to succeed. If nothing happens before sunrise, then return here and we'll try something else.'

Brian borrowed a pair of bull dogs, along with his own two greyhounds, and prepared to wait for the midnight hour. His friend, who owned the dogs, came with him and they arrived at the agreed time. They pitched themselves at the bottom of the large field, hidden behind one of the many old thorn bushes that studded the ditch. They dogs lay down beside them, eagerly awaiting the action to come.

It was a still, dark night. The only sound was the screech of an owl, whirring and hovering over the ivy-covered ruins of Aghaboe Abbey, on the lookout for prey.

The long night passed without incident and they were about to give up when a light breeze began to blow and the morning star was visible over the pinnacle of Sheán Mór. The two men talked about returning to their beds before the dawn broke when suddenly a large hare sprang from the ditch behind them and landed on the ground near them.

She remained motionless for a few moments, then looked around. She began to skip and jump, moving closer and closer to the cows. She advanced to the first cow and began to suck from her for a moment, then on to the next and the next until she had sucked from every cow in the field. The cows began to low in an agitated manner and Brian had to be restrained from attacking her.

'Wait,' whispered his friend, 'when she's heavier, 'twill be easier to catch her and she won't escape.'

And so it was, the more the hare sucked, the more her belly distended. She made her way with difficulty across the field to the gap in the hedge through which she had entered. Just as she passed the spot, the men called out to the dogs and they set upon her.

The hare moved quickly, milk squirting from her mouth and nostrils. The dogs made after her, yapping with the joy of the hunt. Rachel Higgin's cottage came into view and it was clear that the hare was heading for it, though she circled the field to the rear.

Brian and his companion made for the house by a shorter route and were there when the hare appeared, panting and exhausted, with the dogs hot on her tail.

She ran around the house, then made for the door. At the bottom of the door was a small semi-circular opening. She made a leap for it, her head and shoulders squeezed through, but one of the dogs caught her by the rump. She gave a loud, piercing scream and struggled to get free, but the dog held fast. When she finally did get inside, the dog had a clump of her skin and hair between his teeth.

The men burst through the door to find the floor streaming with blood. There was no hare to be seen, but they could hear the muffled groans of a woman coming from the bedroom. They could barely make out the shape on the bed, but they were convinced it was Rachel herself who had taken the form of a hare, stolen the milk from the Costigan's cows and left the cows and the family in a state of misery. Under the covers, the woman was contorted with pain from the wound on her backside, which was still bleeding copiously.

Her family were awoken and they gathered around her as she lay dying. Brian and the other neighbours tried to speak to her but she wouldn't or couldn't say anything. She breathed her last that night, and even in death, her face and her body were twisted in misery.

Brian returned home and reported the events of the night to the old woman. He offered her a reward, but she refused all money. She had never heard of Rachel Higgins, but was pleased that her enchantments had rid the family of her jealousy and power.

She stayed a few days in the house, then took her leave, and she was never seen again in those parts.

Needless to say, the memory of that story and the awful events of that night were spoken about for years. Rachel's family left the area soon afterwards out of shame, or so it's believed. But the ghost of Rachel Higgins can sometimes be seen, in the shape of a huge hare, scudding across the landscape towards her favourite haunts.

Some say the story is fanciful and indeed they may be right, but it does show the respect people had for the power of old women both to do good and bad.

BIDDY
AGHABOE

The fate of women accused of witchcraft or thought to have other-worldly powers was often to die a cruel death by hanging for their 'crimes'. Banishment was another form of punishment. 'She was never seen or heard of again' at the end of a story was also a way of getting rid of a troublesome person.

But there are other stories that reflect well on people's attitude to lone women in County Laois.

Jimmy Fitzgerald, whose family owned the Square Bar in Portlaoise for generations, told me the story of Biddy Aghaboe.

Biddy was very poor and she was blind. She had one cow and she would wander the streets and lanes of the town, back when it was known as Maryborough. Nobody knew how she had come to be there or why she had left Aghaboe, but they got used to her and would give her money and food whenever she needed it. She was always grateful to the people of the town for their kindness to her.

One summer there was a drought in the town and a shortage of water. It caused great hardship and inconvenience. There are many wells in the town, but for some reason they all went dry.

Biddy was walking out along the Mountrath Road one day when her cow started to paw the ground and couldn't be moved on. Biddy began to dig at the spot. She struck water and found a well.

The people were so grateful they named it 'Biddy Aghaboe's Well' from that time on. That well is still preserved. When CIE were building a bridge across the road for the Dublin to Cork railway line they placed a plaque below the bridge on the left-hand side, marking the spot where Biddy's well is.[10]

The people of Portlaoise are now planning to erect an even better commemorative plaque, which will ensure that the story of Biddy Aghaboe and her cow, who saved the town from drought, will live on.

12

KIND,
LITTLE WOMEN

*The little red woman appears in other stories collected
in County Laois, sometimes in very helpful guises.*

In the townland of Colt, a certain farmer rose early one winter's morning to go to the fair at Ballinakill. After he had prepared himself, he got a lantern, and went to the field nearby to get the cattle which he was taking to the fair. It was a dark, bitterly cold morning and the farmer couldn't get the cattle out of the field. He chased them many times around and around. In the end, a little woman dressed in red appeared from under an old bush, and helped him to get them out. She could move at a fair lick and when a cow would attempt to make a run for it, she would chase her back to the herd. She never spoke and when he had them on the road, she disappeared. He had of course to drive them by foot into the fair. All the way along the road, she was waiting at every crossroads and gap, and she helped him to keep the cattle from escaping. When he was near the town, and past all danger, she disappeared and he never saw her again. That was after they had passed Heywood, about one mile from Ballinakill.

*Some years ago, two neighbours living in the townland of Cappanaclough,
set out for a fair in Abbeyleix. They were particularly good friends,
although they were of different religions. This story was collected by
Helen M. Roe in* Tales Beliefs and Customs from Co. Laoighis.

After the fair, when two men had sold their stock, they had more than
a few drinks and were well drunk when they set off for home late at
night. They weren't long on the road when a row started and they
quarrelled over something or other. One of them decided to get out
of the cart and walk home. The other continued the journey alone.

After a while, the man who was walking heard the sound of horses'
hooves coming back up the road towards him. It was his friend,
returning to pick him up. He refused and stubbornly walked on.

It happened a second time. His friend came back and asked him
to get up on the cart, but he refused again.

The third time, the cart stopped beside him and the friend
asked him, in the name of God, to get up on the cart or they'd be
there all night!

So he did, seeing there was something strange going on. They
drove on in silence and then the driver told his companion that each
time he passed Derrykearn crossroads, a little woman appeared beside
him on the cart, took the reins out of his hands, turned the horse
round on the road and forced him back to pick up his companion.

13

MOLL ANTHONY OF THE RED HILLS

'Herbs and plants in raths or dells are collected and used for charms and cures by "bonesetters" or "fairy-doctors".'

Canon O'Hanlon, *Irish Folklore* (1870)

Within the present century, one of these fairy women, who was named Moll Anthony, lived near the Red Hills at the 'Chair of Kildare'. Her reputation as a possessor of supernatural knowledge and powers of divination drew crowds of visitors to her daily, not only from Laois, but many from remote parts of Ireland. They were given a bottle, filled with curative liquid, they were then directed to return homeward without falling asleep on their journey. The bottle was filled with water and a concoction of herbs gathered with certain incantations, near a rath.

At one time, a young woman came looking for a cure for a sick relative and was directed to return home with the magic bottle. She was told to keep her eyes open along the way, but, overcome with fatigue and feverish with anxiety and excitement, the young girl was obliged to rest by the roadside.

No sooner had she fallen asleep than one of the ugliest beings imagination had ever created appeared in her disordered fancies. Arms extended, the spectre seemed ready to clutch her. She screamed and jumped up, still holding the bottle.

After the death of Moll Anthony, her daughter followed the same profession, but without the same celebrity.

It was quite a lucrative calling, this curative power.

14

THE STOLEN CHILD

*The following story about Moll Anthony was collected by
Aine Uí Ciarbhaic. Ballyadams National School. 1927. NFC.*

There was once a man and a woman who lived in Coolyhorgan. They had one child, a little girl. One winter's night they were sitting by the fire and the child was asleep in her cradle.

After some time, they heard what they thought was a bee buzzing in the chimney, an odd thing to happen on a winter's night. Later, when they were going to bed themselves, they checked in on their child, but she was gone. They went to the neighbours, and they all searched all around but not trace of the child could be found.

The man went to see Moll Anthony and told her his story.

Moll Anthony asked him how far the rath was from his house. About a hundred yards, he answered.

'Go there at midnight,' she told him. 'You'll see the hunt coming out. The first lady riding on a white horse will be your child. If you're able to pull her off the horse, you'll have her back again.'

So he went to the rath and out came all the gentlemen and ladies on horseback and there in the middle was a girl on a white horse.

He made a grab at her. She was just like a mushroom in his arms, but he ran so fast, he hardly looked at her. He didn't stop until he ran in the door and there was his own child, safe and sound again![11]

The Stolen Child

15

THE
BACACH RUA

*John Keegan, the poet and writer, was born in Shanahoe in
1816. He heard this story one night from a group of local men.
He wrote the story in a style which was literary rather than
colloquial. I have told it many times and this is my version.*

*I was gratified to meet May Kelly from Cashel, near Ballyroan,
who confirmed the story and told me that her father had worked
on the construction of the bridge and that he used to walk
twenty-five miles every day to get to and from the site, and that
indeed the bridge was completed in less than one year.*

The beautiful River Nore flows through County Laois. Nowadays
there are many bridges built across the River Nore, but time was
when the crossing of a river took place at fords, shallow spots on the
river, where it could be crossed by people and animals without too
much fear of drowning. Shanahoe, outside Abbeyleix, the birthplace
of the Laois writer and poet, John Keegan, was named after one of
these fords. The Irish word for a ford is '*átha*', so Shanahoe is the
anglicisation of '*sean átha*', meaning 'old ford'.

Many years ago, Neil O'Shea and his wife Kathleen lived in
a small cottage beside the ford on the river. Theirs was the only
cottage within shouting distance of the ford. Local people had constructed a 'footstick' across the river, so that travellers could find a

steady path as they made their perilous way across the water with their carts and their animals. This stick would be attached to heavy rocks and boulders to keep it steady and it took skill and knowledge to cross safely. As theirs was the only house within calling distance, many a night Neil and Kathleen would be wakened by a shout for help, if the river was in flood or a hapless traveller chose to risk the crossing after a few drinks too many. In fact, like a lot of women, Kathleen slept with one ear open, in case of a call in the middle of the night.

One wild winter night in November, when the wind was howling and the rain lashed against the window panes, Kathleen was woken by what she thought was a cry of distress. She woke her husband, telling him to 'get up quick – someone is in trouble in the river!'

Neil got up immediately, threw on the big grey coat that was always at the ready, and he went out into the darkness with his long iron-shod stick. When he reached the bank of the river, he called out, over the wind and the watery roar, 'Is there anybody out there?' In the murky darkness he could not see clearly, but then he thought he heard a faint human cry. With his stick to balance him, he made his surefooted way across the foaming water, stepping on the footsticks he knew were there. As he came nearer to the bank, he could make out the shape of a human figure, desperately clinging to a bush, half in and half out of the water. He reached out and with herculean strength lifted the body over his shoulder. He stood and steadied himself and then made his way carefully back to the other side without slipping once. Back in the house, Kathleen was up and busy and making hot tea. She had the fire banked up. Neil brought the soaking body into the room and deposited him on a chair beside the fire. They took a good look at him.

He was a tall, thin man with a face that looked worn, more from hardship than from age. His clothes were ragged and through a tear in his trousers they could clearly see he had a wooden leg. His head was covered with a broad-brimmed leather hat and underneath he wore an enormous nightcap of rough red flannel wool.

But this poor man was weak and wet, and they asked no questions until he was dry and warmed by the hot tea, a supper of brown bread and jam before him and the heat of the fire warming his bones. As they sat around later, the stranger eventually told them his story.

He was from the north of Ireland originally. He ran away to sea when he was a young lad of sixteen and travelled the world in his youth. He was involved in a skirmish with pirates in the Bay of Biscay and lost his leg in the fight. Now a one-legged sailor is useless on board a ship, so he left his job and had to take to the roads. There was no alternative but to ask for any help he could get, and he had depended on the kindness of strangers for the last twenty years. But his luck had almost run out when he was found half dead at the ford and saved by Neil O'Shea. He was alive now thanks to the generosity of Kathleen, whose tea and food had restored him. Kathleen offered him a bed for the night in the 'settle' at the chimney corner, which he gratefully accepted as he was exhausted.

He was up at sunrise next morning and ready to leave when Kathleen took pity on him again. 'Look,' she said 'you've had a hard life, travelling the roads of the world. Why don't you stay here for a while? We have a spare room at the back and we've only the one son, Terry, here with us now. You could do worse than sitting down there by the ford and asking for a few pence from the people passing over the river. The people around here are decent and charitable and I'm sure they would cheerfully help you out if they could.'

The old sailor was happy with the arrangement and every day after that he would sit himself down on a big stone down at the ford. As people passed, he would take off the big leather hat and ask them for a few coppers for the good of their souls. He was rarely refused. Time passed and people got used to seeing him there, with the wooden leg and the outstretched arm and the red nightcap always covering his head.

They named him the Bacach Rua, '*bacach*' being the Irish word for a cripple and '*rua*' because day and night, winter and summer, he wore the red nightcap. The stone he sat on, they called '*Cloch an Bhacadh Rua*', the Stone of the Bacach Rua. In fact, there were people who never remembered a time when he wasn't there. He seemed to have become part of the landscape, sitting on his stone with a greeting for everyone who crossed the ford.

He never washed himself or changed his clothes and people wondered what he did with all the money he had gathered. Kathleen fed him well and he had a bed to sleep in every night. If anyone asked him about the money he'd collected he would rage and swear he hadn't a penny to jingle on a tombstone after he'd paid for his tobacco and other stuff he needed. But if he was spending his money, there was no sign of it anywhere.

The years passed and in time, Neil O'Shea grew old and died and was buried in the nearby graveyard at Shanakill. Nobody lamented louder at the funeral than the Bacach. 'What'll I do without him?' he cried. 'He saved my life and kept me alive. Och, I'm lost without him!'

But although Neil was gone, Kathleen promised that as long as she and her son Terry still lived, there would always be a bed for the Bacach Rua.

Forty years had passed since the Bacach first crossed the River Nore and all that time he was to be found sitting from early morning to night on his favourite stone by the riverside.

One morning Terry awoke and found the Bacach was still in his bed in the room where he slept. He was surprised as the old man was usually first to rise up in the morning.

'Are you alright?' Terry called through the door. There was no answer. Terry looked in and there was the Bacach, stretched out on bed, pale as a ghost with the nightcap on his head, as usual.

'What's wrong with you?'

'Ach, Terry, I'm dying … I've taken a turn and I won't be up again till you lift me into the coffin.' Terry was fond of the old man, who been part of his life since he was a child.

'Can I do anything for you? Will I go for the priest?'

'Ach, no, there's nothing a priest can do for me now. I haven't said a prayer for years and I'll not start now.'

'What about a doctor?' said Terry. 'Give me some money and I'll get the doctor for you.'

'What are you saying? Give you money for a doctor? I've no money! How can I pay for a doctor?' And he let rip such a string of curses that Terry went out of the room. The old Bacach's anger made him upset. The ungrateful old miser was dying and he still wouldn't spend a penny. He went back in.

'Is there anything you want to say to me before you go?'

The Bacach heaved one great sigh. 'Bury me with my nightcap on!'

Terry went out to call his mother and when they came back in the Bacach was breathing his last few breaths.

They gave him a good funeral, as was the custom in those days, and all the neighbours came to pay their respects. They carried his coffin to the graveyard where he was buried with all the dignity they would give to one of their own.

Rumours were rife, of course, about the money they all knew the Bacach had collected over all the years, sitting there by the ford. Where was it? The neighbours assumed that Terry and his mother had got it.

But Terry and Kathleen had not a clue where the money was and wondered even more than the neighbours where he had hidden it.

Terry went to bed that night, but couldn't sleep a wink. He tossed and turned and came down in the morning with deep dark lines under his eyes.

'What's the matter with you, Terry?' said his mother when she saw him.

'I don't know,' said Terry. 'I'm tormented. I see visions of that auld Bacach before me every time I close my eyes.'

'It's no wonder,' said his mother, 'when the misfortunate man died without a priest and a curse on his lips. Tell me though, what is the Bacach doing when he appears in your dreams?

'He's just as he always was, but he has his withered old finger pointing up in the air.'

'To his head, is it?' Kathleen asked. 'Maybe we buried him with a knot or a string tied on the nightcap. It's well known that a spirit won't rest if there is a knot tied anywhere on the burial clothes when the coffin is closed. I'd advise you to go down and make sure or we'll have no peace in this house.'

Terry had no intention of going to the graveyard alone. So he asked one of the neighbours to accompany him. They went to the grave, where the soil over the coffin was still loose. They opened

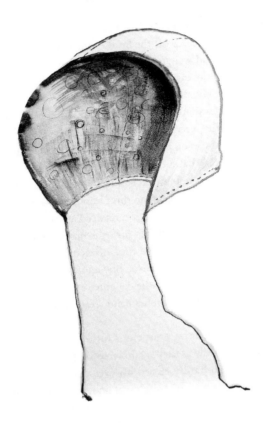

the coffin, the corpse was examined and Terry saw that his mother was right. The red nightcap was knotted tight under the dead man's ear. Terry bent down to unloosen it. His hand shook and he tore a bit of the lining. He did think he noticed something, but he said nothing. He opened the knot and closed the coffin again.

When the neighbour had left he told his mother. 'I think I know now where the Bacach has hidden his money.'

He decided to go back to the graveyard that night, alone this time, with just a spade to clear the earth from the coffin. It was a bright moonlit night as he walked, the only sound the scrunching of gravel beneath his boots. He scraped away the earth from the top of the coffin. He turned the screws and slowly lifted the lid.

The moon shone down on the dead man's face. Terry bent over and quickly whipped the cap off the head of the Bacach. It was heavy, he thought. A dead weight. He closed the coffin and screwed it tight. He spread the earth over the top, then left the graveyard at speed. He walked home along the river bank.

His mother was waiting for him, full of fear and expectation.

'Are you alright, Terry?'

Terry flung the cap on the table. His mother produced a scissors and set to work. What a discovery! Inside the lining of the old woollen nightcap, carefully stitched to conceal and to protect the old man's skull, were no less than three hundred golden guineas.

Joy and ecstasy! Mother and son rejoiced at their good fortune. They sat up for hours, planning how the money would be spent. It would come in handy. The roof needed fixing. They could restock the farm. They could even buy another farm! Terry could approach the girl he fancied, the daughter of a rich man, now that he had something to offer for her hand. Terry was clear about what she could offer him!

There was hope for a prosperous future and mother and son were smiling broadly as they lay down to sleep that night.

But Terry had hardly closed his eyes when the noise started and woke the house. The banging of doors and the tramping and stomping from room to room of a wooden leg. A rattling of cups and plates. A crashing of pots and pans. The dog was barking, the cat was screeching. The ashes from the fire were blown all over the place. It was as if a demon was rampaging through the house, causing havoc.

Terry and his mother were terrified.

'It's the Bacach,' she said. 'He's back and he's searching for his money! We'll have to get rid of it!'

'I want no more to do with it,' said Terry. He gathered the coins up in his mother's old check apron. Next morning at daybreak he ran the two miles to the parish priest's house and banged at the door. When it was opened by the housekeeper, he pushed past her and up the stairs into the bedroom. The priest was sitting up, eating his boiled egg and toast.

'What brings you here, Terry?'

Terry threw the apron of money on the bed and told the priest he could have it. He wanted nothing to do with the miser's money.

'I won't have him tormenting me and my mother, polthogue-ing about the place. You can take the money.'

'I don't want it either,' said the priest. 'What do you want me to do with it?'

'I don't care,' said Terry. 'You can make a bog or a dog or a deal with it.' With that, he ran back down the stairs and away.

Well, within an hour, the Bacach Rua's money was parcelled up in brown paper and was transported on horseback and delivered to the Secretary of the Queen's County Grand Jury in Maryborough, along with a letter detailing the story of how the money came to be in the possession of the priest.

A month later the matter of the money was discussed by the Grand Jury and it was agreed that it would be used to construct a stone bridge across the ford where the money was collected.

Within twelve months of that date, a fine bridge of seven arches was built across the river. From that day to this, the bridge is called the Poor Man's Bridge in memory of the Bacach Rua. Terry O'Shea and his mother were never troubled again. They are long gone now, but local people say that sometimes on a moonlit night, the figure of an old man can be seen on the bridge, his head covered in a large nightcap, and from the sound of his wooden leg thumping the ground, they know it's the Bacach Rua returning to search for his money. Some say more of it was hidden under the stone he sat on, but it was never found, for the large stone was incorporated into the bridge when it was being built.

16

OUR KITTY

*This story was told by a man called Michael Malone
from Rossmore Bog. He called it, 'What is Bred in
the Marrow can by no means be got out of the Bone'.
It was collected by Seosamhín Ceitinn in 1934.*

At one time, there was a very rich lord and his lady, who lived not far from here in a place called Ballyvandan Castle. Now, they had all that money could buy, but there was a certain calamity in that they had no family.

But still, they were peaceable with each other.

After a while, they decided to adopt a child. They ordered the carriage to be got ready and they set out.

After going through Abbeyleix, they went into Portarlington and Mountmellick, but they could find nothing there that suited their tastes, so they changed their course and came south-east.

They took the high road up by Rossmore Bog and along by my place here, until they came to the noted plain called the Platform, where the high road runs parallel through Clogrennan Wood for Leighlin Bridge.

They had only gone a short distance when their attention was drawn to a small child picking wildflowers by a shallow brook that flowed by the wayside. The carriage was brought to a standstill. They went over to where the child was and they questioned her.

They were delighted by her answers and her appearance. She was a lovely child with blue eyes and curly hair.

They walked slowly down the road until they came to a spot called 'Hetz Corner', where the road takes a sharp bend.

There they came upon three or four carts unhitched. A woman on one side of the road was getting food ready for a midday meal. Other women were washing and spreading out the clothes to dry on a hedge.

On the opposite side of the road, some men and boys were at work, soldering kettles, bottoming pots, and making pans, every man with his hammer going whick, whack.

They made known their business and asked if they could adopt the child.

'Oh,' said one woman, 'that's our Kitty.'

They went to her and the bargain was done and the adoption drawn up in a legal form.

The child was bundled into the carriage, then the carriage turned right around and back it went to Ballyvandan Castle again.

Two maids were set aside to attend to her and a governess was brought in to teach her manners in her youthful years. But later, when she grew up, she was sent to a grand high school on the Continent to finish her education. Then she was to come home to Ballyvandan to reside with her parents.

A big celebration and banquet was prepared for her homecoming. All the young nobles and everyone who was anyone was invited.

She stood in the spacious hall to receive the guests and everyone spoke of her beauty, her skin which was as white as the driven snow, her teeth which were as clear as pearls and her hair which fell in golden locks.

After dinner, we were all ushered into a spacious hall decorated for the dance. Everything was perfect. A musician from the west of Ireland played for the dancers. Going around in the waltz one of the young gentlemen trod on her satin gown and it was torn.

She stood like a statue in the middle of the hall. Her eyes blazing, she rolled up her sleeves and swore a prodigious oath that I won't repeat here and said, 'If I had a soldering iron now, I'd mow the head off your body!'

A gloom came over the hall. The dance was brought to a standstill.

My Lord and his Lady were disgusted. To think of all the money they had laid out to pay for the education of that girl!

In disgust and shame they sold their estate at Ballyvandan Castle, went out to live on the Continent and died of broken hearts.

I have never heard tell of what happened to the girl.[12]

17

Stories of
Strange Cats

The Lake of Cats

This tale was collected by Áine Uí Chiarbhaic.
Scoil Seosamh Baile Adhaim/Ballyadams.

There was once a man called Will Duffy, who lived by himself in a cabin on the side of a hill which looked down on Stradbally town. He wasn't well off, but he made his living by cutting hazel and blackthorn sticks and selling them in the town on fair days.

One day, he was sitting down at home having a cup of tea, when in wandered a little *puisín* (a kitten). 'You're welcome,' says Will. 'You can stay here with me and keep me company.'

He went to the dresser, filled a saucer with goat's milk and gave it to the cat. She drank it, lay down by the hearth and made herself at home. Will took out his pipe, had a pull of it, all the time looking at the *puisín* asleep by the hearth. After a while he went out to collect the cows and milk the goats and fetch a sup of water for the night. All the while, he was thinking of going to the fair in Ballinakill in the morning. When he got back in, the kitten was gone.

'*Musha, purshone* to ye for a *puisín*,' he said, 'you're like the rest of the world, an unthankful beast ye are, sure enough.'

He went to bed, slept soundly and was up early the next morning. He opened the door and there was the bould *puisín* and

she sitting outside the door, waiting for him. 'I thought you were gone from me,' said Will.

So, it went on like that for a while. The *puisín* stayed there during the day, was gone at night, then returned the next day.

After a while, Will noticed she wasn't growing at all. She was as small and skinny as the day she came in the door.

'I'm afraid I'm wasting my goat's milk,' he said, looking at her. 'You're not growing a bit. You'll never be a cat.'

Up spoke the *puisín*. 'Let it be known to ye, my people are all small. No, you're dead right. I'll never be a cat, but it's lucky for you, you were good to me.

With that she gave a screech of a *MIEAAUU*. Will near jumped out of his skin and made for the bag that was near the fire. He caught the *puisín* and stuffed her into the bag.

'You're out of here,' he said. 'Whether it's you that's talking to me, or the spirit that's inside you.'

Down he went to the pond in Ballinclea to drown her. Just as he was taking her out of the bag, a *slua* of *puisíní* came out of the pond, leppin' and squeelin' and bawlin' in all directions. Will pelted the *puisín* into the pond and took off. What was the *puisín* but one of the fairies!

The pond has gone by the name of Loch na bPuisín ever since and few would care to pass it, especially late at night.[13]

THE TALKING CAT

This story was recounted by archaeologist Helen Roe in
Tales Customs and Beliefs from Co. Laois. *Irish versions*
of this tale are also in Béaloideas, *Vol.3, p.66.*

There was a farmer driving home to Timahoe from the fair in
Portlaoise. When he came to the crossroads at Money, his cart was
violently tilted up and he looked back to see that a black cat had
jumped in over the tailboard.

The cat was a big one and seemed to be much heavier than it looked. As the horse could not draw the cart with the shafts up in the air, the farmer said to the cat, 'Either get out, please, or come here beside me.'

The cat moved up and sat beside the farmer on the far side of the slat (the sitting board). After a while the farmer got used to having the cat there, but was rightly shocked when he came to the next crossroads and the cat spoke.

'Tell Prettyface that Booman is dead,' it said before it jumped out of the cart and disappeared.

The farmer went home and said nothing at first. He unyoked the cart and gave the horse some oats and hay and a drink of water and then went into the house for his tea.

'Well,' said his wife, 'how did you get on?'

'Fine,' he said, 'I got a good price for the pigs right enough.' He gave her the money and she put it in the tin she kept over the mantelpiece.

'Did you meet anyone?'

'I did, of course,' he said.

'Any news?'

'Divil a bit.'

'No news? Surely to God, there must be some bit of news out there!' She had been all on her own all day and was dying for a bit of news.

'Well,' he said, 'you won't believe this. But I met a talking cat.'

'You did not,' she said. 'You're making that up.'

'I did,' he said, 'he jumped up on the cart and spoke to me.'

'Were you drinking? Are you drunk?'

'I am not,' he said, 'I had a few but I'm not drunk. The cat spoke to me.'

'What did he say?'

'He said tell Prettyface that Booman is dead.'

'What?' said the wife. 'What kind of a thing is that to say!' She shouted louder, 'Tell Prettyface that Booman is dead! What kind of nonsense is that!' Just then, their cat, who was asleep by the fire suddenly jumped up and gave three loud *miaows*!

'Why didn't you tell me! I'll be late for the funeral!'

She ran out the door and was never seen again.

18

THE
TAILOR

*This tale was collected by Áine Uí Chiarbhaic. Baile Adham/
Ballyadams. 1927. NFC. The handwriting in this collection
is so good and the writer is so faithful to the unique
language dialect of the storyteller that it is reproduced as
closely as possible to how it appears in the manuscript.*

There was an oul woman one time, livin' by herself in a cabin at
the end of a boreen. 'Twas seldom she seen anyone, except now
and again a neighbour might ramble in of an evenin'.

This evenin' anyhow, an oul man came up to the door to ask for
lodging for himself and his wife.

'I never takes in lodgers,' says the old woman, 'for I'm alone by
myself, snug and aisy.'

'Ye're a poor woman, I know,' says the oul man, 'but it won't be
long 'til you'll be rich.'

'Why then, you look poor enough yerself,' says she, 'an' that
poor woman behind ye,' says she, pointin' to the wife, 'have no
great cuma o' wealth on her either.'

'Well, me good woman,' says he, ''twouldn't do for us all to be
showing off, but we have full and plenty all the same.'

'Well,' says the oul woman, 'seeing how it's getting late and that
yiz have nowhere to go, I'll give yiz shelter for the night.'

With that, she opened her half door and let them in.

They sat down by the fire and the oul man's wife took out a bag, as what looked like a málín of male (a little bag of meal) out from under her oul cloak, and she laid it down at the hob.

'Could you tell me, my good woman,' says the oul man, 'is there much work to be got for a tailor around these parts?'

'Well,' says she, 'there's a good tailor in this parish and maybe he'd be wantin' a journeyman.'

With that, the oul lad got very vexed and says he, real cross like, 'Be it known to ye, me good woman, that I am no journeyman. I'm a tailor that made clothes for a king.'

'Beggin' your pardon,' says the poor old woman, and she angered like. 'I thought 'twas lookin for work ye were.'

So with that, he pulled out a little bag out of his pocket and laid a weeshy (tiny) scissors an a smootherin' iron an' all the accoutrements that a tailor would have down on the table and every one of them made of gold, though they were no bigger than me little finger, each one of them.

'I'll be makin a new suit for another king tonight,' says he and then put all the little tools together again and put them into the bag.

'I never heard tell of a king around these parts,' said the old woman, real frightened like. So with that, he jumped up and leapt across the half door and out o' sight with him.

'He'll leave us plenty o' money when he has his work done, so he will. Well I can't know,' said the woman of the house, 'how a crippled old man like that could leap out over a half door,' says she. 'Didn't he tell you he was a tailor?' says the wife, 'and a tailor never went out a half door; he always leapt across it. You know a tailor is always very "soople", no matter how ould he is.'

'Well to be honest with ye' says the woman o' the house, 'I don't like the looks of him at all, at all, an' if 'twas daylight, yez'd be going quick out o' here, so yiz would, if he was back this minute.'

The tailor's wife laughed a squeaky little laugh and says she, 'Ye don't know the luck you're in for at all, at all. Only be civil to him when he comes back, for he'll be here at cock crow.'

Begor, when the cock crew, in he leaps across the half door.

'Come on now,' he says to the wife, 'we must be goin'. I'm thankful to you, me good woman,' says he to the woman of the house, 'for sheltering me wife and yez'll find something good in that bag on the hob. An' if you'd like to know who I am, I'm a tailor to the King of the Fairies.' And with that, up with the two o' them like fork lightning up the chimney and away with 'em, out o' sight.

'Musha, purshune on yiz goin',' says the poor oul woman, 'look'd the way, I'm after losin me nights sleep wid yiz.'

So begor, she opened the little bag that was left on the hob and 'twas full of oaten meal and down in the middle of it was a fine lump of gold. The poor oul woman shared her good fortune with the neighbours that used to be good to her when she was poor and in want, but begor, if she did somehow or other, 'twas unlucky, for any wan that got a red penny out of it, 'twas poorer that ever they were in no time for 'twas an oul sayin' that money that's got too aisy is never lucky.[14]

19

CLOPOOK

THE *DÚN* OF CLOPOOK

On a mild autumn day, I set off to find the *dún* of Clopook. I had found a number of references to it in the stories collected in 1927 by Áine Uí Chiarbhaic, a teacher in Ballyadams National School.

I was curious about the strangeness of the name; Clopook, which in Irish is *Cloch an Phúca*, meaning the 'stone of the spirit'. A spirit in folk tales can be anything so I wanted to see the place for myself. Heading towards Carlow through Stradbally, over the Windy Gap and down the hill, and just before the sign for Ballyadams, I took the road to Luggacurran. I came to a crossroads, looked up at the hill on my right, overgrown with thick growth and scrub and signs of an old construction, and I said to myself, 'That's it! *Cloch an Phúca.*' There were two men working on a small house at the side of the road. I asked them where Clopook was. In typical understatement, one said, 'You're not far', and pointed up the hill.

'Is it ok to go up?' I asked.

'Well there's cattle in the field. The man who owns the land lives about a quarter of a mile away beyond the graveyard. You'll probably see him in the field.'

I drove up the lane towards the hill. Rabbits and pheasants scattering before the wheels of the car. I passed the fort on the right and pulled in at the end of the track, where the door of the house was open. I knocked and realised the farmer was having a rest after his dinner. He came out and I asked if I could go inside the *dún*. 'No problem,' he said and showed me where and how I could climb up, by skirting the electric fence and then stepping between the two syca-more trees where there was a rough stone path leading up to the cave.

The path ascends through a tangle of trees and bushes to the most impressive limestone cave into which I had no desire to descend. At the mouth of the cave was a circle of stones and the ashes of a fire. The atmosphere was eerie and compelling.

The farmer, Michael Lynch, was still in the field. The cattle watched with interest. I made my way back, very pleased that I hadn't given up and asked the farmer about the place.

'What is the *púca*?'

'It's a monster rabbit or hare. Some people say it's a woollen fleece. The fleece comes out of its lair from time to time, moves at great speed with a buzzing sound.'

Michael Lynch's family have lived there for generations, but he only recently bought the land on which the fort is situated. He has heard many stories about the *dún* and the *púca*, but takes them with a grain of salt.

Luggacurran, which is across the valley from Clopook, is the site of another cave, where the music of bagpipes has been heard from within. Killone Cave, at the side of a hill, has been described in vivid detail in Canon O'Hanlon's *History of the Queen's County*.

'At first sight the entrance is narrow, dull, dark and dismal with projected rocks, hanging dangerously. However, lit with more light, it displays the most brilliant scene ever exhibited by nature. Painted rocks festooned, and bouquets of pearls, diamonds, rubies, and every other precious stone, in full oriental splendour, caused by drops of water issuing from the calcareous rocks.'

Some weeks later I returned to Clopook with Seán Murray, who, as an archaeologist, has a great interest in the cave. We entered and found ourselves in a dry cavern festooned this time with the cocoons of indoor spiders. There is graffiti on the wall with the date 1884 carved on the rock and the initials 'FHL'.

The cave has never been excavated but there have been a number of attempts to uncover its mysteries. On one occasion, a man dug into the earth of the cave and uncovered a mass of metal. He chipped some away and it was conjectured that it was slag from a Bronze Age smelting operation.

St Fiacc of Sleatty is supposed to have made a pilgrimage from the mountains of Margy to Clopook to fast for the forty days and nights of Lent.

There is a very old graveyard and the remains of a monastic settlement in part of the territory which contains the *dún* of Clopook. A lake in the field where the cattle graze has the appearance of a sinkhole. There is a strange beauty and atmosphere in these parts, as though they hold many secrets, and it is no wonder that many of the stories in the area reflect this.

THE MAGICIAN OF CLOPOOK

The following tale was recorded by Dan Hassett,
De La Salle Brother, Castletown, County Laois.

The *dún* of Clopook was once a great centre of learning. The master at the school, whose name was O'Kelly, had a fine reputation as a teacher and was deemed to be a man of great skill and brilliance. It was believed he was also skilled in magic and divination. Scholars came to the school from far and near. A young man from Wicklow was accepted as a student and his family and friends were proud and pleased for him. However, when he returned home for holidays his friends were surprised to find him so pale, thin and nervous. When asked what was going on, he didn't answer, and seemed reluctant to give much information about the school.

Wicklow is a fair distance from *Cloch an Phúca*, but some of his good friends decided that after the boy had returned to the school, they would follow on secretly and see what was happening. They hid themselves near the school. At midday the boys were let out to play and a very surprising thing happened.

The master suddenly appeared at the door and, with a wave of his stick, he turned the boy into a hare and the other boys into

hounds and there was a lively chase as the hounds pursued the hare back and forth, and up, down and around the *dún*. But just when the hare was at the end of his tether and was about to be caught, the master, with a wave of his stick, changed hare and hounds into human shape again.

The watching friends of the Wicklow boy rushed from their hiding place and, with angry shouts, bore down on the master. He realised the game was up and he was about to be unmasked. He changed himself into a huge cat and ran wildly towards the *dún*, where he disappeared into the cave and was never seen again.

THE ENCHANTED HARE

This was collected by Áine Uí Chiarbhaic, Ballyadams. The Rory O'Moore mentioned in the tale was the leader of the O'Moore clan, the main resistance to British rule in the region from the sixteenth century onwards.

A man went out one evening to shoot rabbits on Tully Hill. He saw a hare and fired a shot at it. The hare ran across the field, crying like a child. The man got a great fright and ran to the house on the other side of the hill, where a farmer, his wife and their three children lived.

He asked the woman if any of the children were out as he thought it might have been one of them he'd heard crying. He was told the three children were fast asleep in bed. He went home and told his uncle what had happened.

'Oh,' said the uncle, 'that's the enchanted hare which comes from the *dún* at Clopook. The hare appears on the hill every seventy years. It's supposed to be a child who died or was stolen by the fairies.'

On another occasion, passing by the *dún* of Clopook, a man heard a sound coming from inside the cave. It wasn't just one voice, but many voices. He couldn't make out a single word that was spoken. It was like music to his ears. He went to a local house and told his story. People there laughed at him, but an old woman sitting be the fire, said, 'Ah, you poor *garsún*, look what you missed now, not being able to speak your own language. They were speaking Irish and all the people who used to understand them are dead. Their leader was Rory O'Moore himself!'[15]

20

CAOCH
THE PIPER

If you couldn't sing, play a tune, dance or tell a story in the days
before television in Ireland, then you could at least do a recitation.

'Caoch, the Piper', as recited by Benedict Kiely, was well known to
radio listeners in the 1960s and 1970s and was also included in
school readers. It is John Keegan of Shanahoe's best-known poem.

'Caoch' means blind and blind pipers were not uncommon.
Music was always a way for a disabled person to make
a living, travelling the roads providing entertainment
in return for food and a bed for the night.

One winter's day, long, long, ago,
When I was a little fellow,
A piper wandered to our door,
Grey-headed, blind, and yellow –
And, oh! how glad was my young heart,
Though earth and sky looked dreary –
To see the stranger and his dog –
Poor 'Pinch' and Caoch O'Leary.

And when he stowed away his bag,
Cross-barred with green and yellow,
I thought, and said, 'In Ireland's ground,
There's not so fine a fellow.'
And Fineen Burke and Shane Magee,
And Eily, Cáit, and Mary.
Rushed in, with panting haste to see,
And welcome Caoch O'Leary.

Oh! God be with those happy times,
Oh! God be with my childhood,
When I, bare-headed, roamed all day
Bird-nesting in the wild wood –
I'll not forget those sunny hours,
However years may vary;
I'll not forget my early friends,
Nor honest Caoch O'Leary.

Poor Caoch and 'Pinch' slept well that night,
And in the morning early
He called me up to hear him play
'The wind that shakes the barley'.
And then he stroked my flaxen hair,
And cried – 'God mark my deary',
And how I wept when he said, 'Farewell,
And think of Caoch O'Leary.'

And seasons came and went, and still
Old Caoch was not forgotten,
Although I thought him dead and gone
And in the cold clay rotten.
And often when I walked and danced,
With Eily, Cáit, and Mary,
We spoke of childhood's rosy hours,
And prayed for Caoch O'Leary.

Well – twenty summers had gone past,
　　And June's red sun was sinking,
　　When I, a man, sat by my door,
　　Of twenty sad things thinking.
　　A little dog came up the way,
　　His gait was slow and weary,
And at his tail a 'bocach' limped –
　　Twas 'Pinch' and Caoch O'Leary!

Old Caoch! But ah! how woebegone!
　　His form is bowed and bending,
His fleshless hands are stiff and wan,
　　Aye – Time is even blending
The colours on his threadbare bag –
　　And 'Pinch' is twice as hairy
And thin-spare as when first I saw
　　Himself and Caoch O'Leary.

'God's blessings here,' the wanderer cried,
　　'Far, far, be hell's black viper;
　　Does anybody hereabouts
　　Remember Caoch, the Piper?'
With swelling heart I grasped his hand;
　　The old man murmured, 'Deary!
　　Are you the silky-headed child,
　　That loved poor Caoch O'Leary?'
'Yes, yes,' I said – the wanderer wept
　　As if his heart was breaking.
'And where, *a mhic mo chroí,*' he sobbed,
　　'Is all the merrymaking
I found here twenty years ago?' –
　　'My tale,' I sighed, 'might weary,
Enough to say – there's none but me
　　To welcome Caoch O'Leary.'

'Vo, vo, vo!' the old man cried,
   And wrung his hands in sorrow.
'Pray, lead me in *a stór, mo chroí,*
   And I'll go home tomorrow.
My peace is made – I'll calmly leave
   This world so cold and dreary,
And you shall keep my pipes and dog,
   And pray for Caoch O'Leary.'

With 'Pinch' I watched his bed that night,
   Next day, his wish was granted;
He died – and Father James was brought,
   And requiem Mass was chanted –
The neighbours came – we dug his grave,
   Near Eily, Cáit and Mary.
And there he sleeps his last sweet sleep-
   God rest you! Caoch O'Leary.

21

FOUR SAINTS AND THE BOOK OF LEINSTER

The tradition of visiting holy wells on the pattern (from 'pátrún', meaning 'patron') day of the saint associated with the wells has not died out. Brigid, Patrick and Colmcille may have been the most popular at one time, but the stories and tales of many other saints of Ireland are as imaginative as any wonder tale; a mix of fact, fiction and folklore.

SAINT FINTAN

St Fintan was very influential in the area which is now County Laois. He is one of the patron saints of the county. Others include St Colman of Oughaval and St Mochua of Timahoe. He founded a monastery at Clonenagh, *Cluain Eidhnach,* the Ivy Retreat, which is situated on the road between Portlaoise and Mountrath. The site of the monastery was of such importance that it stretches across a wide area, now cut through by a very busy road between the two towns. It is well worth a visit for the views of the surrounding landscape, as much as for the ancient stones which have been unearthed in the construction of a path in the newer part of the site.

It was believed that anyone who was buried there would be fast-tracked into heaven. The graveyard near Fintan's church also contains three large mounds, one of which is associated with St Brigid of Kildare.

There is an interesting story of how St Fintan settled in
Clonenagh. He was originally a student of St Columba in the monastery at Terryglass, and when the time came to move on, both he
and Columba came to Clonenagh. But they found no peace there,
so many were the visitors passing along this busy roadway and
staying, drawn by the presence of the two holy men. So they decided
to move nearer the mountains of Sliabh Bladhma, the Slieve Blooms.
While they were there, they met a herder named Setna, who was
dumb. Columba blessed him and he was cured. When he began to
speak, the Holy Spirit inspired him to tell Fintan and Columba to
return to Clonenagh and to build a monastery there.

There was a fine spring well near one of the religious houses.
This well was a place of great veneration among country people.

In the nineteenth century, the owner of the land was a
Protestant. He was annoyed at the number of people who visited
the well, so he decided to fill it in. By some extraordinary power,
attributed to the saint, the well sprang up on the other side of the
road in the trunk of a sycamore tree. The water rose in a hollow in
the tree to a height of about ten feet above the road. People would
climb up onto the tree to make a wish with the water and tie a rag
or a piece of a ribbon to the branches of the tree. They then began
to hammer coins into the bark of the tree as a form of votive offer-
ing. It was known as the Money Tree. Some years ago, poisoned by
the metal from the coins, the tree fell down.

However, when I visited it recently, the well at the base of the
tree was still evident and there were signs that new shoots were
growing from the old branches. It is still a place of devotion on
St Fintan's pattern day on 17 February.

Fintan's rule was very strict and it was said that he lived on bread
of barley corn and earthy water. One day when he was crossing a
field carrying a bucket of water, he stumbled and the water spilled
out. On the spot where it touched the ground, another well sprang
up at Cromóg.

This well, on the other side of the town of Mountrath in the
direction of Abbeyleix, is also dedicated to Fintan. The well is not
easily found without local knowledge. On the day I went to seek

it out, with Seán Murray, a young archaeologist from Portlaoise, we were directed down a boreen by two young boys who were walking their dog along the road.

It was 17 February. The road to the well was very well maintained, with rough handmade signs showing the direction. The shrine surrounding the well was encased in glass and the brickwork on the wall was very neatly constructed and held cups with which to draw the holy water. A bullaun stone stood beside

the lively stream which flows from the well and on the spring day on which we visited the water sparkled and tasted like the freshness of a new life.

Collect water from this well and your house won't go on fire. A pebble collected from close to the well will also protect your house. A local RAF pilot who fought in the war was known to always fly with a bag of these pebbles in the cockpit. He was never shot down.

There is said to be a one-eyed trout in this well. If you see it, your wishes will be granted. The story of the trout is as follows. A local woman brought her kettle to the well to be filled. When she went home and set the kettle to boil, no matter how hot she made the fire she couldn't get the water to boil. She plunged a fork in to see if there was something in the water and stuck the fork in the trout's eye. She returned with the kettle, the water and the trout still inside, and emptied the water back into the well. To this day, that trout has one blind eye.

SAINT BRIGID

They say that St Fintan met St Brigid one time when they were both looking for sand and gravel to build their respective monasteries. Fintan was digging sand from the Downs, the esker ridge at the edge of present-day Portlaoise, near where the large Catholic church stands today. St Brigid asked for some of the sand and Fintan refused. They got talking and maybe recognised something in each other's way of speaking. It turned out they were both from the same clan, the Fothairt people of the north-east. When they knew each other's seed, breed and generation, Fintan agreed to share the sand with Brigid and he sent her off with a cartload. This story cannot be verified historically, but it is interesting that one of the burial mounds at Clonenagh bears the name of St Brigid.

Another time at this same spot on the downs, Fintan lost his temper with people who queried his right to take the sand. He hit the ground with a stick and a holly tree grew up at the spot.

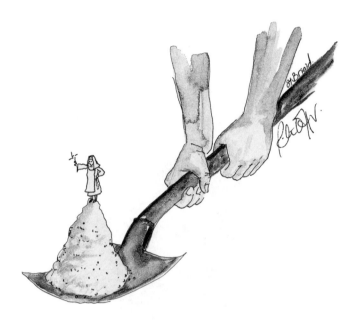

It is believed that St Fintan returns to earth every Christmas and celebrates Mass at the altar of the old church at Clonenagh. No one has ever seen the Mass, but it has been heard. People claim to have seen the ghost of his horse galloping over the downs.

SAINT FIACC

St Fiacc, who was a bard before he became a Christian, was credited with introducing the Latin alphabet to Ireland.

His mother was a sister of Dubhtach, the chief bard and brehon (judge). Fiacc was apprenticed to Dubhtach and began his studies to carry on the family tradition. When Patrick came to convert the Irish, he headed first to Tara and asked permission to address the powerful bards and the Druids. They exercised such an influence on the people that he needed them on his side. He wanted to explain the beliefs of Christianity to them first.

St Fiacc of Sleaty — Rob O'R 2015

King Laoghaire, the High King, asked the bards not to stand for this newcomer. Dubhtach and Fiacc showed him respect and did stand.

In fact, Patrick, on his travels, visited the home of Dubhtach at Donaghmore in Laois. The story goes that Patrick spoke so well and impressed them enough that they embraced the new beliefs. Dubhtach was the first convert to Christianity and Fiacc the second.

Fiacc didn't have a wife and, as the younger of the two, was ordained. It is said that it was Patrick himself who cut off his beard and gave him the tonsure.

Fiacc set off to find a spot for his monastery. He first went to the east side of the River Barrow in Carlow to found his monastery but sixty of his monks died of a wasting disease. He moved to the west side after a series of visions and it's there in County Laois that the ruins of the monastery lie today at Sleatty (*Sléibhte*).

It is believed that he learnt the Latin alphabet and went on to write in manuscript form the first life of St Patrick.

Legend has it that he walked from Sleatty to the *dún* of Clopook on a pilgrimage and that he prayed for forty days and nights inside the cave there during the Lenten Fast. It can't have done him any harm because it is believed he lived to the ripe old age of 105 years. He died in AD 520.

(Information on St Fintan and St Fiacc came from Laois archaeologist Sean Murray and Helen M. Roe in Tales, Customs and Beliefs from Laois.*)*

Saint Mochua of Timahoe and his Three Pets

The lives of the saints in Laois are embroidered with myth and lore as is illustrated in the story associated with St Mochua, who gave his name to the lovely village of Timahoe (*Teach Mochua*). He was a warrior from the west of Ireland, who converted to Christianity and the monastic ideals of simplicity and prayer. His monastery in Timahoe dates from the seventh century.

St Mochna
& his three pets

A magnificent round tower, in perfect condition, attests to the building skills of later monks and the need to protect the treasures and manuscripts of the monastery from the marauding Vikings.

The story of Mochua and his three pets is well-known locally.

Mochua and Colmcille of Iona lived at the same time and were close friends. Mochua lived very simply as a hermit, with no worldly goods, except for three pets: a cock, a mouse and a fly. The cock woke him for prayers. The mouse let him sleep no longer than five hours and, if he slept longer, weary as he was with all his vigils and prostrations, the mouse would lick his ear until it woke him. The fly's job was to walk along each line of his psalter as he read it, then stay on the exact spot he finished on, so he knew where to pick up again when he came back.

Now, one by one, each of these three precious pets of Mochua died very soon after each other. Mochua wrote a letter to Colmcille in which he told of his sorrow at the death of his flock. St Colmcille's reply was to the effect that this is what happens when you have too many worldly possessions.

'My brother,' he said, 'marvel not that your flock should have died, for misfortune ever waits upon wealth.' Hardly a sympathetic response.

SAINT COLMAN AND THE BOOK OF LEINSTER

A short distance outside Stradbally on the Carlow Road there is a spot which was known as Tulach Mhic Comhgaill. It is now more commonly known as *Ougheval* or, in English, Oakvale.

Ougheval was the monastery founded by St Colman in the sixth century. Colman was a descendant of Lughaidh Laoiseach, which would have made him one the O'Moores of Laois. Others say that he was a member of the Bardic clans, the McCrimmons.

The story goes that as a devout young man Colman went to Iona to join the monastic settlement of Colmcille. He was lonesome there and couldn't forget his native land. He confided his state of mind to his spiritual master. Colmcille understood loneliness, as he was an exile from his own native place, Doire (Derry).

He advised Colman to return to Laois and to go to Fintan of Clonenagh, whom he had seen in a vision standing among the angels in the tribunal of Christ every Sunday. Fintan would become his *anam chara* (soul guide).

Colman did as Colmcille suggested and studied with Fintan in Clonenagh. He then went on to found his own monastery in *Ougheval*.

His death is recorded in Adamnan's life of Colmcille …

St Colman

One night Colmcille had a dream that Colman had died. He saw him being taken from this life by a host of angels. He stopped all work the following morning and told his monks and followers to keep the day as a holiday for Colman who had died during the night. They did this and celebrated Mass in his memory of his passing on to another life.

Later a messenger travelled to Iona to tell of Colman's death. Colmcille had got the day and the time right!

The monastery was sacked by the Danes in the ninth century. In their hasty flight from *Ougheval*, it was believed that the monks hid the sacred vessels in a well near the abbey. Up until recently, there were people living in Stradbally who could point out the exact situation of the well, which was covered over. One elderly woman remembers a game the children would play, jumping on the flagstone which covered the well in order to hear the jingle of the metal underneath. There is a belief that bodies buried at Ougheval do not decay as quickly as they do in other parts.

THE BOOK OF LEINSTER

Historians of medieval Ireland believe that Leabhar na Núach-ongbála/The Book of Ougheval, now known as the Book of Leinster, comes from Stradbally, although some say it was written in Clonenagh and then moved to Ougheval for safety.

Among the pieces contained in the Book of Ougheval are: the oldest copies of the Dinnseanchas, the legendary account of the origin of various names, places, rivers and lakes in Ireland; the Fate of the Sons of Uisneach; fragments from the Táin Bó Cúailnge; numerous other pieces in poetry and prose; and a vast collection of Irish lore.

The manuscript is now at Trinity College Dublin, but at one stage it was in the hands of a man named Roger Moore, who turned out to be none other than Rory O'Moore, who was associated with one of the many rebellions against the English in 1641. It is also believed that it was the O'Moores who had a hand in the creation of the book for, as Johanna O'Dooley, a local historian and storyteller, says, before the invention of print 'every monastery, every princely family, and even individuals kept huge books of parchment in which to note historical data and treasures of oral literature worth preserving'.

It is due to the work of the scribes, who worked so diligently on these manuscripts, that stories were kept alive in Ireland. When the bards of Gaelic Ireland were no more, it was the storytellers and the *seanchaithe* in the houses and cottages all over the country who kept the stories alive by telling and retelling them at night by the fireside for entertainment and diversion during the long winter nights.

The Curse of Saint Patrick

This tale was collected by D. Hassett, FSC.

Uí Duach is an ancient territory division in Leinster. It lies mostly in present-day County Kilkenny but is partly in County Laois. Some of the present-day place names help to fix its location to some extent. Names such as Doonane, which in the Irish language is *Dúnan na nDuach*, and Durrow, which in Irish is *Darmhagh na nDuach* are in present-day County Laois. But Firoda, which bears the Irish form *Fir na nDuach*, and Three Castles, which is *Bán na nDuach* in Irish, are all in County Kilkenny. The countryside through which the River Dinín flows in north County Kilkenny is known as *Fásach Dinín* now, but at an earlier period it was called *Uí Duach*.

After St Patrick had descended the valley of the River Barrow with the intention of going to present-day Kilkenny and into Munster, he found it necessary to cross into ancient *Uí Duach*. But immediately he came up against the hostility of the inhabitants. Their hostility took the form of stone-throwing and we are told the saint reacted with some impatience, crying out, 'I curse, I curse *Uí Duach. Mallachtím, mallachtím Uí Duach.*'

But one of St Patrick's followers, who was a native of *Uí Duach*, added, '*Bíodh sin ar dhíon na gcruach.* Let that fall on the haystacks.'

The curse of St Patrick

But St Patrick repeated, 'I curse, I curse *Uí Duach. Mallachtím, mallachtím Uí Duach.*'

But again the *Uí Duach* man answered, '*Bíodh sin ar bhárr na luachra.* Let that fall on the tops of the rushes.'

But St Patrick continued, 'I curse, I curse *Uí Duach. Mallachtím, Mallachtím Uí Duach.*'

However, the *Uí Duach* man was still there and he added, '*Bíodh sin ar an Dinín Ruadh.* Let that fall on the Red Dinín.'

After that St Patrick seemed to have cooled off and the rest of his sojourn in the territory was happy. The curse of St Patrick must have had some effect however, because the stacks of hay and corn are more frequently demolished by turbulent winds in the area than elsewhere, the tops of the rushes are usually withered and the Dinin River, as everyone knows, is subject to devastating floods.

22

THE MAN FROM LAOIS
WHO BECAME POPE

This comes from a Historical and Social History
of Durrow *by Edward O'Brien.*

There is a legend among the people of the Aran Islands concerning an abbot of a monastery on Inishmore who became Pope and Bishop of Rome. St Benedict, one of the most famous of the early Irish saints, was born in Durrow, County Laois. He was the son of the King of Ossory and although he could have succeeded his father and claimed the title, he chose to study under St Fintan at Clonenagh.

While he was there, he formed a bond of friendship with Colmcille, who was also well connected as he was one of the great clan of O'Neill from the north-west of Ireland. After their ordination both went to the monastery founded by Naomh Éanna on Inishmore.

The next years were spent in prayer. Colmcille went on his mission to Iona and Benedict became the *anam chara*, the soul friend of Éanna.

In AD 522 Benedict and Éanna went to Rome. While they were there, Pope Hormisdas died. Being struck by the piety of Benedict, the man from Laois, the assembly of elder bishops and clergy elected him as successor. He took the name of Pupeus.

According to the legend, on the following day, Éanna came to say his farewell. The parting was too much for the new pontiff.

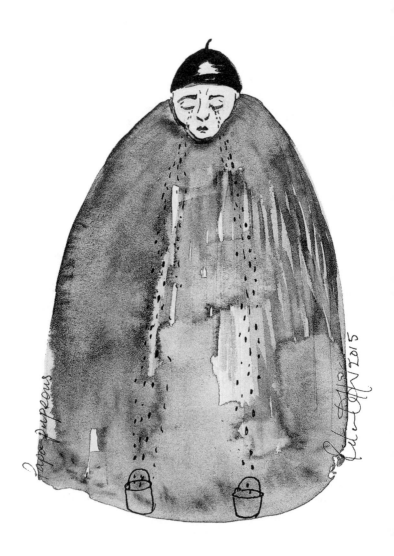

He summoned the assembly of Church leaders again and ordered that another election take place. On this occasion Pope John I was elected.

Éanna and Benedict returned to the Aran Islands. After Éanna's death, Benedict succeeded him as abbot. They are buried side by side in the graveyard of the monastery, which is now in ruins. Both feast days are on 21 March. The Book of Cashel, which traces the genealogy of the fourteen saints of Ossory, refers to St Benedict as '*Ipse est Papa Pupeous*' (He is the Pope Pupeus).

23

THE WHITE LADY
OF DURROW

One summer evening some years ago there were two boys playing hurling on the GAA pitch in Durrow. The sun was going down and they pucked the ball to each other as they often did before it got dark. One of the boys had a small little terrier dog who accompanied them whenever they were going to the hurling field. The two boys were pucking away when suddenly the dog became very agitated and began to bark incessantly. This was very unusual behaviour for the little terrier as he was normally of a placid nature, preferring to lie at the back of the goalposts until the boys had finished their play.

The dog ran onto the clay bank that surrounded the playing field and continued yapping its incessant little bark. They muttered, 'What the hell is wrong with that blasted dog?'

They decided to investigate the cause of the agitation.

As they ran up the clay bank towards the dog a white flash, which lasted a few seconds, appeared before them. 'Did you see that?' one asked.

'I did,' said the other in bewilderment. They looked into the obelisk field surrounding the GAA grounds, which was part of the Ashbrook Estate, but there was nothing to be seen. No cattle, no dogs, no rabbits, nothing. They were young lads and they had never heard the legend of the White Lady.

The River Erkina, a tributary of the River Nore, flows through the town which grew up around the estate at Castle Durrow.

In 1708 the lands around Durrow were 'released' to William
Flower Esq., a son of an English officer, and his heirs forever by
James, Duke of Ormonde, for a sum of £68 3s 4d with three
fat beeves (oxen). William Flower built the mansion at Durrow
and received the title the Baron of Castledurrow. His son Henry
became Viscount Ashbrook and so the titles and land passed
from father to son in the manner of the aristocracy. William,
the 2nd Viscount Ashbrook, was a young man who was being
educated in England, as was the custom.

One day he and his pal wanted to go fishing in the River Isis at Oxford. It was customary at that time to seek the services of a ferryman to take fishermen across the river to the best fishing location. But the ferryman on this occasion was nowhere to be found so the daughter of the ferryman, a strikingly beautiful girl of 16 years, agreed to take them across the river on the boat. In the course of the day's fishing, young William was enchanted by her beauty and was smitten by a *coup de coeur*!

Her name was Elizabeth Ridge and he fell madly in love with her. Nothing would satisfy him but to marry her, despite the fact that, as a ferryman's daughter, she was well below his station and class. An arrangement was made with her father John Ridge to send her away to be tutored privately in etiquette, good manners and behaviour, as befitted the duties of the wife of an Ashbrook. This she did and after three years the couple were married. Elizabeth then came to Durrow, well prepared for her role as viscountess. It is said that William erected the obelisk which stands across the river from the castle as a tribute to her, though his mother thought he was doing it to improve the vista. Elizabeth was energetic, handsome and charming and was well liked by the people of Durrow. She gave birth to five daughters and two sons.

Then tragedy struck. One of the little girls, at 8 years of age, fell from a horse and was killed instantly. The death shocked Elizabeth, as did the death of her husband soon afterwards at the age of 34. William's father had died at a young age, as did his son, also named William, who succeeded him. And so it seems that bad fortune pursued the family down the generations as long as they had lands in County Laois.

Some time in the 1940s there were two young lads playing along the backs of the River Erkina. They were walking home when one of them realised he had forgotten his coat and went back to collect it. He saw a ghostly figure in white, lying against the stone bridge which crosses the river Erkina adjacent to Castle Durrow.

He grabbed his coat and ran. He too had seen the ghostly presence of Elizabeth Ridge. More often, she is seen from a distance, riding a white horse on the high ridge across the river from Castle Durrow, near where the famed obelisk stands.

The legend still inspires people who live in this lovely town. The local drama group is actually called The White Lady Drama Group and in 2014 they staged an imaginative outdoor production of The Ferryman's Daughter, *which was staged in promenade-theatre style in Durrow. It is fitting that that final act in the production was played out on the grounds of Castle Durrow, once the home of Elizabeth Ridge, the White Lady of Durrow.*

24

THE BALLAD OF
JAMES DELANEY

*I heard this ballad at a session in a pub in Borris-in-Ossory
on a windy night in November 2002. It was sung by Martin
Delaney and he introduced it as a true story which took
place in Rossbawn near Ballaghmore in November 1858.
It concerns the shooting of a man called George Ely, who
was the agent of the landlord Sir Charles Coote. Ely had
accused James Delaney of poaching when, as Martin
put it, he was out shooting rabbits to feed his family.*

*There are different versions of this ballad and in some versions
the landlord's agent is named Richard Ely. However, all
of them share the local sentiment that James Delaney was
doing nobody any harm and the threat of the eviction
of his father was unjust. The song tells the story.*

Information from this tale comes from the Midland Tribune, *June 2003.*

My name is James Delaney
And I'll take my pen in hand
To write you down a line or two
That you might understand

For I've been young and lighthearted
I carelessly strode on
To amuse my prime
In the summertime
With my dog and gun.

'Til one of these cursed traitors,
George Ely called by name,
Maliciously reported me
For hunting on the game

And when the landlord heard of this
All tenants he did call
For every man to pay his rent
All men, both great and small.

My father, he being the first
Who went to pay the rent,
He shouted out to Delaney,
I'm glad to see you here

For I am told and will enfold
Since you came to this town
Your son's a daily hunting
With his gun and hounds

And I am told and will enfold
And much do you I blame
To allow your son
His dog and gun
Go hunting on the game.
Oh, well bespoke the father
These words to him did say:
I swear before your honour
It was unknown to me.

I beg your honour's pardon
In what I'm going to say
I fear you are mistaken, sir,
A kindly led astray

If that be so, Delaney, then
I'll gladly try the case
And I will bring another man
To meet you face to face.

George Ely, he being called upon
To force up this great ban,
How dare you propose a lie
To such a worthy gentleman.

When young Delaney heard of this
The blood boiled in his veins
To seek his satisfaction
What e'er might be his fate.

'Twas in George Ely's body
He lodged a fatal ball
And brought him down
Unto the ground
All in his crimson gore
And ne'er to rise and tyrannise
The lands of Ballaghmore.

'Twas over his dead body
An inquest they did hold
There were doctors and coroners
And jury men, I'm told.

No blood money could they subdue
His life to swear in
From different parts of Ireland came
A band of Orangemen.

Farewell unto Hibernia,
Likewise my Shamrock shore;
Farewell unto my sweet Rossbawn,
I must leave and see no more

I now must leave my parents,
'Twas them I did adore,
For the shooting of a kite
On a November night
That flew through Ballaghmore.

The fate of James Delaney after the event varies. Local tradition has it that James Delaney went into hiding immediately after Ely's death and was harboured by local people in the border area. It's understood that he emerged only at night-time and managed to lead a secret life for several years. When he died his body was interred in secret at night in Kyle cemetery.

Another local story recounts that the constabulary were waiting for the fugitive at his home in Rossbawn, but as Delaney approached the house his sister warned him off by throwing a ball of wool out the window and he made his escape.

Despite a large reward being put up for Delaney's capture by landlords from Laois and the surrounding counties, no one provided information as to Delaney's whereabouts.

Newspapers of the time, which virtually all represented the interests of the landlord class, were scathing in their condemnation of people who harboured Delaney.

Police were quartered in Ballaghmore to try to capture Delaney but to no avail. In 1860 it was concluded that he had made his escape to America and the force was withdrawn.

His family, the Delaneys of Rossbawn, played a key role in the 1798 Rebellion and six brothers helped capture Cloncourse Castle. However, their daring deed had horrific consequences as all six were hanged by British forces on Rossbawn Hill.

25

BLOODY BATTLES

It is almost impossible to separate story from history. There was an intense awareness of the past in the stories I heard from the people of Laois. It's hard to avoid the tales of the bloody battles which were fought in the Midlands in an attempt to resist the presence of the English settlers in territories that had once belonged to the Gaelic chieftains. Yet many of these settlers are still in Laois after nearly 450 years and they, too, have stories to tell.

Adrian Cosby still lives at Stradbally Hall, the ancestral home of the planter family whose story is intrinsically interwoven with the story of Laois. The estate is now run by his son Thomas as a working farm and a business, and is the location for the annual end-of-summer arts and music festival Electric Picnic and the Stradbally Steam Rally.

The Cosby family built the village of Stradbally to house the workers and craftspeople who worked on their estate. They were responsible for setting up the flour mill and the malting house, which also provided work for many of the inhabitants. The nearby quarry supplied the limestone for many fine buildings, including the present Stradbally Hall.

When Adrian was a young lad at boarding school in Eton, he was shocked when someone from Stradbally, who was working in the house he was living in, told him in terror that his ancestor

Francis Cosby used to have a priest for breakfast every day. Ludicrous as the story seemed to him, it shows the fear and hatred which existed between the two sides fighting for control and power in this strategically important part of Ireland.

The treachery behind the massacre which took place at the rath at Mullaghmast in nearby County Kildare is still part of folk memory.

The Gaelic clans of Laois were invited to a friendly gathering on New Year's Day 1577 by some of the leading planter families, led by Francis Cosby and Robert Hartpoole. The 'parley' was to be amicable and the invitation was taken up in good faith by 400 men who entered the rath. Instead of a feast many were slaughtered in cold blood by the English troops under Cosby on that fateful day.

One of the leaders of the O'Lalors, Henry Lalor, suspected something was amiss. He had watched hundreds going in to the rath, but none had come out. He left some of his followers outside and entered cautiously. A terrible spectacle of slaughter met his eyes and he realised that they had innocently walked into a trap. He fought his way out and escaped, knowing that the carnage would continue. And so it did, with the Cosby's forces laying waste to the castles and homes of the dead leaders.

Henry Lalor's young wife and two small children, one a babe in arms, were at home in the castle at Dysert Aengus, near

Stradbally. They were alone, apart from an elderly herdsman. When they heard the sound of horses' hooves coming towards they house, the old man took the baby away into the hills to hide him but the young mother and her three-year-old daughter were slaughtered and the child was left hanging by the hair of her head from the gatepost.

The little baby, who was brought by the herdsman to his mother's people in Orchard, near Timahoe, survived. His name was Mathew Lalor.

When he came of age, he was the man who defeated and killed the infamous 'Séan a' Phíce', John of the Pike of Ballyadams Castle. He then married another Lalor, named Catherine. Their daughter Elizabeth married James Malone. Their daughter Mary married Michael Dunne. Their daughter Elizabeth Dunne married Sean O'Dooley of Lismore in Waterford. And it was their daughter, Johanna O'Dooley of Stradbally, who told me the story. This is a story which came down through the generations to this remarkable woman, who is in her eighty-sixth year as I write.

Johanna has a humorous and pragmatic way of remembering the past and the struggles for power that went on. 'In my opinion,' she says, 'Francis Cosby and Rory O'Moore were two of a kind. If either of them were against you, your goose was cooked!' But the memory of the blood-sodden soil of Mullaghmast is still there in the stories and they say that the curse of the widows and orphans after Mullaghmast can last seven generations.

There were many more battles in the Stradbally area, which was an important part of the Queen's County, situated as it was on the road from Portlaoise to Carlow.

Even now, there are local stories about the Battle of Stradbally Bridge in 1596, where Owney Mac Rory Og O'Moore challenged the Cosbys for the right to cross the bridge over the River Straid at Stradbally. The O'Moores and their warriors were led by the blood-curdling sound of drums and warpipes played by the hereditary pipers, the McCrimmins, who were the pipers to the O'Moore's. The younger Cosby took fright at the sight and sounds of the warriors approaching but his father restrained him and told him to 'face the music'.

Father and son, Alexander and Francis Cosby lost their lives in
that skirmish. Their respective wives Dorcas Sydney and Eleanor
Hartpoole are reputed to have watched the fighting from their
home at the abbey and were said to have argued about which of
them was widowed first and thereby entitled to inherit the estate.
The abbey was burned down and the women escaped. Eleanor's
baby son William was carried to safety by one of the maids.

To avenge the deaths of the two men, ten years later, William's
uncle Richard Cosby challenged the O'Moores to a battle at
Aghnahily, near Dunamase. This time, the Cosbys were victorious
and seventeen of the O'Moore men died.

Then in 1607, an agreement was brokered whereby the leaders
of the Septs of Laois were to be transported to lands farther along
the Shannon (Tarbert in north Kerry) and the lands of Laois were
left to the English settlers. Not surprisingly the 'agreement' did not
stick. By 1610, unable to prosper in the wet boggy lands of Kerry,
many began to sneak back, preferring to die in Laois than to live
somewhere else.

The O'Moores refused to be sidelined. They were 'loyal' to the
Crown when it suited them, but would rebel again when they
figured the time was right. It was another Rory O'Moore who led
the rebellion in 1641.

I sat by the fire on a cold winter's evening with Adrian Cosby,
who is now retired from farming, and listened to him speak about
the long line of ancestors who went before him. His memories of
being put on a pony at 6 years of age are amusing. 'It was rather
alarming!' He never enjoyed fox hunting, even though he would
drive his elderly mother around to follow the hunt. 'It's more of a
chase really; the fox usually is cleverer than the hounds.'

Our conversation is a reminder to me of how the family we are
born into shapes our destiny and how we tell stories to make sense
of it all.

Adrian speaks of his great-grandfather Robert Ashworth
Godolphin Cosby with a certain amount of admiration and
regret. This man was responsible for the complete rebuilding
of Stradbally Hall in 1868. He carried out an effective drainage

scheme on his lands, which was widely praised. He built part of the Maltings and many houses, barns and terraces in Stradbally. He kept racehorses, which did well, and restored the lake, which is now open to the public. He became Deputy Lieutenant and stood for Parliament from 1880–1885, but he wasn't elected.

'Great-grandfather Robert died rather tragically in 1920. The family were reluctant to return to Ireland for a time after that. It wasn't safe to live there. What happened was, Lloyd George held a meeting in Portlaoise (then Maryborough) to decide whether they should make peace with the rebels or grouse-hunt the entire country. Many of the landed gentry at the time were old and frightened at the surge in nationalism and the support for Sinn Féin throughout Ireland. Great-grandfather had had his dower house burnt down and he was afraid they would burn Stradbally Hall. So he signed the agreement to make peace, albeit reluctantly. Hamilton Stobbart was just back from the war. He claimed the agreement was contrary to the Oath of Allegiance to the Crown and walked out of the room. My mother's father was the agent here and he drove my great-grandfather home. He was very upset. Next morning he shot himself. My aunt had just brought him his breakfast and she heard the shot as she was coming down the stairs. That was how he died. It was a crisis of conscience.'

Adrian went on to tell me that at his funeral, his coffin was carried by the men who worked on the estate all the way up to the family burial crypt in Ougheval Cemetery, which overlooks Stradbally. These men then looked after the house and estate, keeping the gutters cleared and doing other things so everything was kept in good order until the family were ready to return.

It could be said that the story of Stradbally and the Cosby family, which began 450 years ago, has come to a peaceful point finally. Now, at the end of summer for the last ten years, the parkland of the estate has been transformed by lights and music into a magical playground for the people who attend Electic Picnic.

I am grateful to Johanna O'Dooley and Adrian Cosby, both natives of Stradbally and good storytellers, who helped me piece together the complex tale behind those bloody battles, now thankfully in the past.

26

FRANK FOGARTY
AND THE
PASS OF THE PLUMES

Frank Fogarty lived in Ballyroan and spent forty years of his life working as a tailor. In the past, tailors would travel from area to area. They would stay in a local house, work from the house and then move on. For this reason the tailor was a good source of news and gossip and was often a good storyteller. Frank had a great interest in history but had no time at all for legends and folklore. 'In search of our history,' he said, 'you come across more legends than history. Fairies, banshees, leprauchán s, spirits and ghosts … I suffered agonies because of them when I was a child. I'd be terrified. I'd be listening to them before I went to bed. An uncle of mine would come down from Blandsfort and stay up all night telling those stories and we couldn't sleep after them. Myself and my brothers and sisters, we'd wake up crying during the night. And a lot of people believed in these fairies and ghosts, they did. If a house fell down they'd say it was built on a fairy pass. If they were going to the fair to sell cattle maybe, at Ballinakill, and they met a woman with red hair on the road, they'd go back home. Then there was witchcraft. People were able to take butter and take your crops maybe out of the fields. On May morning, these people would go to the well and skim it and drink it and they were able to take your crops or a cow if you had one. I don't believe it. I believe it's all nonsense, the outcome of the pagan practices of years ago!'

Frank told me in graphic detail the story behind the Battle of the Pass of the Plumes, *Bearna na gCleití* in Irish, which took place on 15 May 1599.

Elizabeth I, the Queen of England at the time, was very fond of Robert Devereux, the Earl of Essex. She sent him over to Ireland to curb the rebellious Irish. He was to go north with his troops to take on the O'Neills, the O'Donnells and the Maguires in Ulster, but instead he went south to Kilkenny to subdue the Munster Geraldines.

Essex had little regard for the Irish, whom he called rogues and naked beggars. They fought in long leather coats with bare legs. However, he later changed his view of the Irish as a result of the Battle of the Pass of Plumes.

He had approximately 2,500 foot soldiers and 260 horses with him. The huge army took the road to Stradbally through the pass of Áth Dubh (the black ford). They camped at Cobbler's Hill outside Stradbally and from there brought provisions into the garrison at Maryborough (Portlaoise). They then moved on back to the road and camped for the evening at the foot of Crushy Duff Hill.

From the top of the hill, Essex had a bird's-eye view of the countryside beneath him, across the plains of Ballyknockan and Cashel. He could see among the forests, bushes and bogs the activities of the men of the O'Moores and the O'Byrnes, led by Owny O'Moore. They numbered only about 500 men, but they had local knowledge of the land.

The next morning Essex and his army set off again down through the mountain pass. The pass Essex had to squeeze his army through was very narrow, with the edge of Bog of Allen on one side and the Cullenagh mountain on the other. His army tried to spread out, up the side of the mountains and into the bogs but they discovered was that the locals had planted 'calthrops' made by blacksmiths to spike the horses. Many of the horses were shod with ironplated horseshoes that could withstand the spikes (examples of these horseshoes were found in houses locally afterwards) but despite this many of the soldiers were forced to dismount.

A combination of the terrain and the calthrops meant that when Essex's army was attacked by the Irish clans between *Móinín na Fola* (the Little Bog of Blood) and *Bóthar na Muc* (the Road of the Pigs) they were unprepared and unable to gather into their battle formations. The encounter was fierce and many men were killed. Estimates of the number of dead vary greatly, depending on who is reporting the story. Some say Essex lost as many as 500 men.

When Ned Duff's house at the crossroads was knocked down in 1834, cartloads of human remains were exhumed when they were digging out the foundations.

The colourful regimental plumage of Essex's horses were strewn around during the battle and blown across the countryside. Local people gathered up the colourful feathers when they found them later on the lands and kept them in attics as souvenirs of the battle.

It is generally agreed that despite the huge army of the Earl Essex, and despite the great losses on both sides, the British were defeated by the O'Moores and the O'Byrnes, who could retreat and hide in the safety of the bogs and hills.[16]

The Battle of the Pass of the Plumes is remembered today by a monument at Cashel, which was erected in 1999, 400 years after the event. The story has passed into folklore and legend.

In his history of the Queen's County, Canon John O'Hanlon remarks that, 'Most of the English historians, Fynes, Moryson, Camden, Lingard are silent on the subject, but local tradition is eloquent on the Battle of the Pass of the Plumes.'

JIMMY DUNNE AND THE THISTLES

Jimmy Dunne lived near the Pass of the Plumes. His grandmother used to say to him, 'Jimmy, a mhic, you should see the thistles at the Pass! Some day soon you'll see a great sight.' Lo and behold, one day at dinner time, Jimmy's grandmother called him again …

In the field under the house, a great *sidhe gaoithe* (fairy wind) blew all the thistles' seeds up in the air.

'Them's the feathers out of the bonnets of the Saxons that your ancestors laid low below in the Pass,' his grandmother told him. And more poetically she went on, 'Them's the feathers that turned into fairies,' she said, 'and they carry on their meanderings every year like that! Up with them in the air for a while, showing off like the Saxons, and down with them to the ground again, and you'd think by their actions that every one of them was a living being and every year I watched them like that in the harvest time. They have to fly!'[17]

27

THE BATTLE OF THE BUTTON, WHICH LED TO CLONTARF

This story comes from Cogadh Gaedhel re Gallaibh
*('The War of the Irish and the Foreigners'), translated by
Revd Todd, 1867. Royal Irish Academy.* Dublin and Local
Irish Legends *by Lageniensis (Canon John O'Hanlon).*

Before the Christian era, the territory of Laois had no separate existence. It was part of Laighin, the Kingdom of Leinster.

The roads went southwards from the Hill of Tara, the seat of the High King, towards *Bealach Mór* on the southern slope of the Slieve Bloom Mountains. The road from the north was known as *Slí Mór* and road from Tara was known as *Slí Dála*. These roads were the equivalent of motorways now and it was said that they had to be wide enough that no group was forced to give way to another so that a chieftain and his army, and a bishop and his followers could pass on the road without either side stepping back.

In AD 1012, Mael Mordha, the King of Leinster, set out to visit Brian Boru (meaning 'Brian of the cattle tribute') at his *dún* (fort) at Kincora, near Killaloe in County Clare. He was carrying tributes of masts from the chieftains of Leinster, Uí Faeláin, Uí Fáilghi and Uí Muireadaigh. On the way, he had to cross the Slieve Bloom Mountains to get to Munster. As he was ascending the boggy mountain, the king reached out to steady a mast. He was wearing a silken tunic that Brian, who was then king of Munster, had given him. The tunic was bordered with gold and with silken buttons. One of the buttons broke with the exertion of holding the mast. When they arrived at Kincora, Mael Mordha took off his tunic and it was brought to his sister Gormlaith to sew it on. She was a fiery lady of whom it was said:

'She took three leaps that no woman had taken before:
A leap to Dublin,
A leap to Tara,
And a leap to Cashel, the rock plain which surpasses all.'

Her leap to Dublin was to marry Olaf, the Viking king of Dublin. She had a son by him, Sitric Silkenbeard, who succeeded his elderly father as king. Her leap to Tara was to marry Maelseachlain, the King of Tara, who was defeated by Brian Boru. Her third leap was to marry the king of Munster, the selfsame Brian Boru.

Brian's ambition was great. He named himself Imperator Scotorum, the Emperor of the Irish.

At this stage, Gormlaith was no longer his wife, but was mother to his son, Donnchadh. She took the tunic from her brother and flung it into the fire.

'Why are you yielding to Brian? Your father and your grandfather never would. And mark my words, Brian's son will demand the same from your son!' Brian's favourite son Murchadh (by yet another wife) was playing chess in the room at that time. He sniggered and one insult led to another. Mael Mordha left in a huff and Brian sent a messenger after him to stop him. At the plank bridge at Killaloe the messenger caught up with him, but Mael Mordha gave him a blow, which broke all the bones in his skull and sent him back to Brian, bleeding.

He then set off back to *Cúige Laighin* to gather his followers. There would no more tributes to Brian. From then on, Brian Boru's enemies were Leinster's friends. Gormlaith encouraged her son Sitric Silkenbeard to persuade Sigurd, the Norse king of the Orkneys, to join the men of Leinster in the fight against Brian.

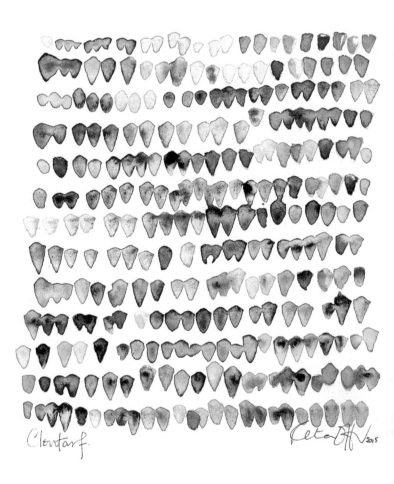

Clontarf.

Brian gathered his troops from Munster and wherever else he could find them before setting off for Leinster. When the army was ready in the springtime of AD 1014, they set off. They spent the first night at Kilabban in Laois. Then they camped on Slieve Margy Mountains and plundered Leinster as far as *Áth Cliath* (Dublin). They laid waste the monastery at *Cill Maighnéan* (Kilmainham) and on Palm Sunday they camped on *Faiche Átha Cliath*, the plain of Dublin, overlooking the city. The plain of Dublin is now the site of the Royal Hospital, Kilmainham.

The forces of Leinster, under Mael Mordha, combined with Viking warriors who came in warships from the Hebrides and the Isle of Man. They fought a bloody battle on the seafront at Clontarf. The battle began on Good Friday, 23 April, AD 1014, at daybreak. By sunset, when the tide was high again, it was all over. Thousands were killed in the carnage, including Brian Boru, his son Murchadh and Mael Mordha, the King of Leinster. Sitric, the Viking king of Dublin, watched the battle from the ramparts of the town with his mother Gormlaith and his wife, who was the daughter of Brian Boru.

The rest, as they say, is history. The Vikings were defeated and the men of Munster, under Donnchadh Mac Briain, began the long march home across the mountains towards Kincora. The bedraggled troops passed through the borderlands of Ossory. At Athy they rested and washed their wounds in the River Barrow. Then they moved on across the country, not realising that the men of Ossory lay in wait, ready to ambush them. Messages were sent demanding hostages or else. Though weakened and wounded, the Munster men would not give in. They hammered wooden stakes into the ground and prepared to fight with one hand, leaning on the stakes with the other. The Ossory men, impressed by their courage, took pity on them and let them pass. The place where this event occurred is still called Gortnaclea, meaning the 'Field of the Stakes'. It's about two miles outside Aghaboe.

Gormlaith, you may be interested to know, outlived her three husbands and her son Sitric. She died in AD 1030, still a proud woman of Leinster. Some say she may have been buried in the vault of Christchurch Cathedral but, being a woman, the place of her burial was not marked.

28

TALL TALES FROM TIMAHOE

THE ENCHANTED FUNERAL

From the 1937–38 Schools Collection, NFC, this story was related by James Quigley (87 years old), Corrigeen, Laois.

The tale I am about to tell happened a long time ago. In this part of the world, there were a lot of tenant farmers who rented from the landlords in those days. There was a fine boy named Ned Tierney who had no one except his widowed mother. Ned and his mother hadn't much money either, but they made the best of it.

At that time, there was a family of the name Bowe living in a house in Kyle. There were five daughters in the family. Lamberton is on one side of Borenamuck and Kyle is on the other.

Borenamuck (*Bóthar na Muc*, the Road of the Pigs) is the road on which the Earl of Essex led his troops to conquer the south of Ireland. O'Moore ambushed them at a place called Pass, up against Ballyknockan Castle. That night all the Pass was covered with Plumes, so it's called the Pass of the Plumes to this day.

There were big sheep farms each side of Borenamuck and those five girls had the privilege of gathering wool from the brambles, which they would add to the wool sheared off the sheep.

They used to wash the wool, card it, spin it and knit it into socks. Every fortnight they would have a gamble, which was when cards would be played for money and the prize would be whatever was up 'for the gamble'. The girls would set up the socks at 1s 6d a pair. Ned Tierney and the other young lads would gamble for the socks.

About eleven o'clock at night, he was returning home after winning about four pairs of socks. He was within three fields of his own house when he heard a noise behind him. He looked around and saw a coffin on a board and only three men carrying it.

Ned was very brave and he said he would help them. None of them spoke a word to him after that, nor he to them.

There was a chapel in Churchtown and a cemetery and Ned thought they were going to bury the corpse there. They passed on until they got to a stile and the first two men got over it. Ned turned to the other man and said, 'In the name of God, how will

the enchanted funeral

you and I get over it?' When he mentioned the name of God, the coffin immediately fell to the ground. The lid flew off the coffin and a lovely girl with golden hair rose up out of it. She told him not to be afraid, that she was not dead at all.

She asked him if he could take her to some warm house because she was cold. He took off his coat, put it around her and took her across the fields to his mother's house. When he reached the door, he shouted in, 'Mother, do not light the lamp and don't be afraid of anything you see.' Ned built up a great turf fire and sat the girl in front of it and they gave her refreshments. Ned was still in doubt about whether she was living or dead until he saw her eating.

She said to Ned, 'My funeral will take place at eight o'clock tomorrow morning. The lane is one mile from my father's house to the road and if it reaches the road, I will be dead. But if I had a young fella who would go from this to that and be there again at eight o'clock to meet the funeral on the lane and make them leave the coffin down and tell them there's no corpse in the coffin at all but a broomstick and a few stones, I would live to be a very old woman.'

Ned asked her where it was. She told him it was in the King's County in a place called Ballanvalley. 'Bedad,' Ned said, 'I think I will go.'

Ned put on a pair of his Sunday shoes, tightened his belt around his body and put on a frieze waistcoat. He left his coat around the girl and went out the door, his stick in his hand. He got into a trot and he never stopped that trot until he reached the lane leading down to Ballanvalley.

When he was down the lane a bit he saw the funeral starting from her father's house. At that time there were no hearses at all; the coffin was borne on men's shoulders. Ned ran up to meet the funeral saying, 'Thanks be to God I am in time.' He took a hold of the bearer, saying, 'There is no body in that coffin at all.' He was pushed here and pulled there but Ned held on to the bearer, saying, 'The girl is not dead at all.' In the end the bearer laid down the coffin and the lid was taken off. Ned threw out a few stones and a broomstick. Everyone gathered around, astonished. They all wanted to know where the corpse was.

Ned threw himself on the grass. He couldn't speak, so he pointed to his mouth and they brought him refreshments.

Then he told them all that took place the night before.[18]

A LEGEND OF FOSSY

The events of this tale happened in the year 1832 or 1833.
It was related by James Quigley, Corrigan, Timahoe,
for the 1937–38 Schools Collection, NFC.

There was an old woman by the name of Susie Bradford who lived between Esker and Timahoe. She had a bag of hazelnuts gathered and when she was nearing her end she gave instructions that when she died this bag was to be placed under her head in the coffin.

At that time, Fossy church was a Protestant church and when a person was buried in the graveyard two men would be told to watch the grave for nine nights. This was because 'sack-'em-ups' would steal the corpse out of the grave in those days as doctors would pay £5 for every corpse the 'sack-'em-ups' brought them.

Soon after Susie was buried in Fossy, another coffin was interred there and the two men were told to watch over the grave. Mick and Paddy were the names of the two men left to look after the

legend of Fossy

grave. Paddy said to Mick, 'There are great fat lambs over beyond in Clashboy and I will go over for one of them and we'll have a great feast.'

'If you do,' said Mick to Paddy. 'I will rise the bag of nuts at Susie's head.'

At the same time, the Minister Booker called his boy to send him down for a book he had forgotten in the church. This minister, the unfortunate man, had never walked a step for seven years before that. When the boy arrived at the churchyard gate, he heard someone cracking nuts upon a tombstone. As fast as he came down, he went back twice as fast and when he arrived back, the minister said he wasn't long. 'Have you the book?' he said.

'I have not,' said the boy.

'Why?' said the minister.

'Because the Devil is below cracking nuts upon a tombstone!'

'Get away,' said the minister.

'Well,' said the boy, 'if you don't believe me, you can go yourself.'

'How can I go when I can't walk?' said the minister.

'Well,' said the boy. 'I can carry you.' The boy got a white sheet and tied the minister to his back and carried him down.

They came as far as the church gate. They could hear the crack, cracking of the nuts against the tombstone. 'STAND,' said the minister, 'he is there sure enough'.

When Mick saw the figure in the white sheet on the back of the boy, he thought it was Paddy coming back with the lamb.

'Have you got him? Fat or lean?'

'Here he is for you!' The boy threw the minister off his back in fright. The minister, who hadn't walked for seven years, ran home and got there before his boy. And the boy went back home and, strange to say, he never entered a Protestant church after that.[19]

The first Mass that was offered in the Church in Timahoe was offered up for the Revd Booker.

MICKEY ROBERTS, THE NECROMANCER

A necromancer is someone who has studied the black arts. People believed necromancers to be in league with the Devil.

The Slieve Margy range of hills straddle counties Laois and Carlow and contain a cross-section of people, some of whom are the descendants of those who were forced to leave the fertile Laois lowlands during the Laois-Offaly plantation of 1556. Others have Welsh ancestry, their forebears having come in the seventeenth century to work in the coal pits as colliers. Others are descended from the Yorkshire pit engineers and managers who came over at the same time.

All these people mixed and married and developed a culture all their own, which included creating a very practical mix of entertainment and commerce, which was referred to as 'the gamble'. This was basically a card game, which involved playing for something useful and desirable, such as socks, in the story above from James Quigley, or fowl or, as in the story related in John Headen's recitation, a 'bushman's' saw.

This handmade saw was much sought-after so there was no shortage of card players at the gamble at Rowan's public house at Knocklaid. The game was twenty-fives and was well advanced when it was interrupted by the notorious Mickey Roberts, whose exploits in the community were feared because it was believed he dabbled in the black arts and was in league with the devil. He had the power to change stones into pigs and back again and to have spades and tongs and pokers hopping and dancing if he wanted to. He used to ramble around at night and people had a terror of him calling in. But he would never be turned away for fear of what he might do.

Mickey asked to join in the game. He was told it was too far advanced, but he insisted and they let him, more out of fear than enthusiasm.

In no time he had caught up with the rest of them.

The cards were dealt for the last time and clubs were trumps. The men looked at their cards and then turned them downwards

on the table to count the game. Having done this they took up their cards and began to play, but to their great astonishment their cards had changed colours and there was not a single trump in their hands. Mickey Roberts led with the ace of diamonds and there was no one to beat him. The neighbours then stood up and went out the door to their homes as quick as they could.[20]

*This story was the inspiration for the following song/
recitation by John F. Headen of Spink, County Laois.*

There is a gamble in Rowan's now the word went around
Three twenty-fives for a 'bushman' that cost a full pound
Finish up the old jobs now and be there for eight
The last gamble in Rowan's ended rather late.

Eight of us came there on a cold winter's night
Maggie stoked up the fire, Mickey turned on the light
The *poíteen* was poured and the pipes they were lit
The cards were then boxed and down we did sit.

Long Mickey Moore and Bill Carroll from the Hill.
Joe Lalor 'the quack' was there with his card-playing skill
Bill Delaney was there and his stook of a son
There were two of the Codys and the bould Paddy Dunne.

The cards they were dealt and we started to play.
Joe Lalor he robbed, so he soon had his way
The gallery it was great for the *poíteen* was raw
The night that we gambled for Mickey Rowan's saw.

The clock it struck twelve when a knock came to the door
Mickey Roberts walked in and plonked himself on the floor.
The card-playing just stopped as we all gazed in awe
The night that we gambled for Mickey Rowan's saw.

Now Mickey was famous as ye very well know
For the powers that he had from the lad down below.
His black magic and art 'twas said had no flaw
That night at the gamble for Mickey Rowan's saw.

We told him to wait while our game did advance
He said no, he was playing and would take his slim chance.
Afraid of disasters and of his black law
We let him play at the gamble for Mickey Rowan's saw.

In no time at all Mickey was going for the game
The cards were put down to check the count was the same
When the cards were picked up a different colour we saw
The ace of red diamonds. Mickey Roberts won the saw.

'Change into a fiddle, saw!' Mickey did cry.
He sold it next day at the fair of Athy.
If you are a fiddler and a bow you do draw
You could be making your music on Mickey Rowan's saw!

THE ROUGH TEACHER

Timahoe, situated between the Hill of Fossy and Cullenagh, is a very attractive village, with monastic ruins, a lovely square, the Bauteogue River and the perfectly preserved round tower, which features an ornate Romanesque door on the first floor. How that was created is a wonder. This was clearly a place of great learning and artistry.

However, like many villages throughout Ireland in recent years, Timahoe has suffered the loss of local amenities, such as shops, the post office and the petrol station. Arthur Kerr, known as Attie, was the local shopkeeper whose corner shop closed in 2011. His was a third-generation business and he still has his grandfather's accounts from the 1890s.

Attie remembered stories about a teacher, named Brown, who taught in the two-storey school in the square in the early part of the twentieth century. Many stories were told of this man and his cruel behaviour towards the children in his care.

There was no water in the school and one day a boy was sent out to the pump on the square to get water. While he was there, one of the local neighbours came over to speak to him. The boy politely continued the conversation, not realising that the master was watching him from the top-storey window of the school. When eventually he returned with the full bucket of water, the teacher took it and poured the water over his head. Then he sent him back to the pump to get another bucketful.

The teacher used to send the children out to work in a field at the back of the school, where they would dig and plant vegetables for the sole use of the teacher himself. The children resented this and thought of a plan to avenge the cruel and mean treatment.

They dug a hole, then filled it with the contents of the outdoor toilet. They covered it loosely with light sticks and twigs and leaves.

They waited until one of them managed to provoke the teacher cheekily. The teacher made a lunge at the bold student, who ran into the garden. The boy skirted the hole, but, by pretending to trip, managed to trick the teacher into making a shortcut over the sewage trap, into which he fell, much to the glee of his pupils!

In another fit of anger, the teacher picked on three boys, whom he considered to be troublesome. As a punishment and to teach the others a lesson, he locked them into the school and went off.

The three boys managed to escape by climbing through the window and shimmying down the drainpipe, but not before they took some lighted sods of turf from the fire and placed them in a circle on the wooden floor.

The teacher returned an hour later to release the boys only to find smoke billowing from the windows of the school. It was he who learned his lesson.

This story was told to me by Arthur (Attie) Kerr.
It is almost a parallel story to the tale of the bullying teacher
in the story, 'The Magician of Clopook'. The dún of Clopook
and Luggacurran are not far (as the crow flies) from
Timahoe. Stories travel and on the way they grow wings.

I'm happy to report, however, that there is a bright
and vibrant new school at the edge of the village,
where learning and the arts are cherished.

29

A STRANGE
FOREBODING

A column of stones now marks the spot where the Hogan family used to live in the Upper Cone (sometimes called Cones), near the source of the River Barrow, on the Ridge of Capard.

They lived on an open green space far from any road or track. With eighteen children, theirs was a large family and their house must have been one of the most isolated in Ireland. Anything they required had to be carried across the mountain as no vehicle could go there. As the children grew up, they left home and went to live here and there until only one boy was left in the place.

Another boy was employed in the town of Mountmellick.

One night, as this lad lay in bed, he had a dream about his brother living in Upper Cone. He dreamt he saw a dog go into the house and immediately afterwards the roof fell in and his brother was killed. The boy in Mountmellick woke up in a terrible state of alarm and although it was the middle of the night, he got up at once and set off for the house in the Upper Cone. It was a long, hard journey along the riverbank and up the mountain. At length, he reached the house and found his brother asleep in bed. He woke him up and told him about his dream. The brother laughed and told him he had made the long trip up the mountain for nothing. However, he got up and made a meal for the Mountmellick boy. Then he said he would go back part of the way with him.

The boy from the Cone whistled for his dog and they set off. They hadn't gone far when, for some reason, the dog bounded back and disappeared into the house. He was no sooner inside when there was a roar like thunder and the roof fell in.

Owen Clear heard this story from his father and passed it on to Brother Dan Hassett, who had made his way to the Clears' house on a wild day on the mountain. The remains of the houses are still there for walkers to wonder how people managed to survive in such a wild, bleak and boggy place. In fact there was a village there that consisted of fourteen families who had been evicted from the

big estate in Capard. They managed to survive by ingenuity, hard work and the old *meitheal* system, whereby neighbours worked together as a team. '*Ar scáth a chéile a mhairean na ndaoine*' is an old Irish expression, meaning that people live in the protective shadow of each other. The Lalors, Fitzpatricks, Conroys, Dooleys, Clears, Hogans and Bowes were some of the families that lived there. There was a tradition that the fire should never go out. It was always kept blazing and if people moved house they would make sure to bring a lighted sod of turf with them to keep life in the place they moved to. The spring well from which the Barrow flows is said to have created the shape of a cone on the mountain where the people found shelter and it is from this that the place got its name, the Cone.

They grew corn, oatmeal and potatoes along the fertile bank of the Barrow. A mill, built by a man called Gallagher, the land agent for the Piggotts of Capard House, was on hand to grind the corn and oats, so there was no shortage of meal or bread.

At the top of the mountain, where the bog was shallow and high grass grew, they could keep geese and cattle.

The last family to live there were the Clears and it was Michael Clear, the nephew of Owen Clear, who told the story above and who gave me an insight into how these hardy people survived.

30

TALES FROM CADAMSTOWN

Cadamstown is a very pleasant village at the foot of the Slieve Bloom Mountains, with the Silver River flowing through it. Paddy Heaney is a native of Cadamstown and his home beside the old mill is a favourite stopping place for people interested in the history, folklore, nature and customs of the area. Paddy has a prodigious memory and many of his memories are included in his book, At the Foot of the Slieve Blooms: History and Folklore of Cadamstown. *The following tales also come from this book.*

I was born and reared in the village of Cadamstown but my ancestors came from Glenleitir Valley about three miles south of the village here.

My grandfather was born in a place called Barr na Scáirt and when I heard people talking about Barr na Scáirt, I thought it was a wonderful place until I rambled up there, stood on a hill and looked down on the valley. Whoever gave it the name knew what they were talking about as Barr na Scáirt means the tops of the bushes. I could see nothing only bushes and furze. I often wondered how families lived there because in the 1871 census there was twenty-seven Heaneys living in three houses in the one yard. There was twelve families living up in the valley. If you stand on the mountain road, above at Heaney's Bridge, which my grandfather built in 1850, you'll see green patches on the sides of the hills. That's where people lived: Kennedys and Quinns and McCormacks and Kilfoyle and Corrigans. The old people remembered the names of the people and places. They were never recorded and but for the old people, they were gone.

When I was young, there was no television, no radio. It was during and after the war years. There was no electricity across the area at the time. Everybody had the oil lamp on the wall and the open fire. When oil would be scarce, we often learned our lessons by the light of the fire.

I can still see the old kitchen, with the open fire on the hearth and the big flagstone. The ramblers used to come in, three, four or five every night, and sit around. We youngsters had little small stools to sit on. My father used to sit on the corner, over near the fire. He was a great pipe smoker. He used to leave his pipe on the hob.

I'd see him lighting the pipe and handing it around, to Mick Carroll, Pat Purcell and Henry Manifold, like the Indians. They'd smoke and then hand it back. Then someone else, after an hour, would do the same. You'd always know when a story was about to unfold, because my father would take up the tongs and prod the fire.

Maybe it's what they used to see in the heart of the fire, I don't know. But that's when you'd hear the way of stories. We had a big bend – the 'lasair', my mother used to call it – where she'd keep her oatmeal to keep it warm. There was a form (wooden bench) along beside it. That was our first stage. We were all involved in music. My father had a set of pipes, which he brought home from America in 1921. They belonged to Patsy Tuohy, a famous Galway piper. When visitors would come, or when all the youngsters from around the village would come in, he would sit up on this chest, put his feet on the forum. The idea of that was because he was afraid anybody would hit against the drones or regulators. If a visitor was there, he'd have to explain about the pipes and how they worked.

Around the fire, that was my university because I learnt so much there.

Pat Purcell, his father, Mick Purcell, was involved with the Fenians. Mick Carroll was an engineer with the North Tipperary County Council. He used to live at the back of the church. He used to come down every night. He was a Gaelic speaker.

Henry Manifold, he was descended from the Cromwellian planter. Henry was a great storyteller as well. He was well educated because the big houses that time used to employ teachers. So Henry was taught at home in the big house. He was also taught in a hedge school in Glendolan. My father often pointed out where Tobias Chambers, and John Chambers and William Chambers, came from. They were all hedge schoolmasters.

My grandfather was taught by them.

THE BLACK MAN OF O'CARROLLS' CASTLE

Just across the field where we are sitting now is MacAdams Castle. One branch of the O'Carrolls of Ely settled in the Castle in the twelfth century. The O'Carrolls built the castle. They were chiefs of the area and were beginning to push out the small man. One of the O'Carrolls was Thomas, known as Black Tom. He lived there in the castle. He wasn't so well liked. He didn't get a good press.

The story was that when he left, he buried money somewhere in the vicinity of the castle. He was killed later in the Jacobite Wars.

This was often discussed around the fire. Now, it was around the time of the Fenian Rising in 1867. A lot of the fellows around here were involved. They used to come in here to our house, along by the road. It was a long, thatched house. It was right beside the police barracks, the remains of it are still there. The police would always ramble in. Not that they were welcome or anything, as my father used to say. They'd be rambling in to hear what was going on. But when they'd come in the chat would stop.

Jimmy Ryan it was who made the pikes.* He owned the pub and he made pikes for the Fenian Rising, which took place in 1867. The pike heads were buried in the gardens around the village. The police knew there was something going on, but they couldn't put a finger on it. But still, they were on the alert. So Mick Egan, Mick Purcell and Henry Manifold concocted a plan.

They were all rambling in our house one night when Mick Purcell arrived in. After a pause, he said he'd had a dream that there was money buried in the old castle at Ballymacadam.

'Before you can do anything about it,' said my grandfather, 'you'll have to dream twice more!' The police sergeant was there, Sergeant Monnelly, listening as usual. After a week, Mick came in again. He was after dreaming a second time. After a few more nights he came and said he had dreamed the third time and he knew exactly where this money was located.

Henry Manifold said, 'We'll get a team together and we'll dig for the money.' Mick Purcell said it wasn't as easy as that because there was a black man guarding the money. Black Tom Carroll. So Henry said they'd have to pick a good team. They did that. Henry Manifold, Mick Egan, Mick Purcell and Dan Guilfoyle. They agreed on a night, when the moon would be full and they would go out at twelve o'clock. So on the night they agreed on, they all arrived with crowbars and spades and shovels and Tommy Davi, who owned the shop on the far side of the pub, came over with a bottle of whiskey. Sergeant Monnelly came in. He was trying to make a laugh of the whole episode.

They all kept very serious. About ten to twelve, they shouldered their implements and they marched out the road. Before they left, they said someone should remain in the kitchen, that they'd be back in an hour. My grandfather said he'd remain. The police were walking up and down outside, on duty. An hour and a half passed, then two hours. Then they heard a noise coming from down along the road and they saw these lads coming along and they were carrying a gate and Dan Guilfoyle was lying on it and they had him covered with a frieze coat.

All the police came out of the barracks, asking, 'What's going on here?'

Mick Purcell explained that they were digging for the money and they were just down three or four feet when they hit something, like metal. The next thing, the black man came out of the ruins of the castle. 'We tried to keep him out of the hole, but eventually a storm rose and we had to fly for our lives. Dan Kilfoyle got the worst of it, so we had to carry him home.' They brought Dan in and they gave him some whiskey to revive him. Dan came to after a while. This took three or four hours. But Sergeant Munnelly then told them that it was better they all go home and forget about the episode. They all went home right enough.

It was on the following day when people saw the horses and sidecars coming from Birr and Kinnitty, manned by police. They dug up every field and garden and searched every shed in the area. They were looking for weapons. They arrested the men suspected of being in the Fenian movement.

They eventually found out what had happened during the night. While the big drama in O'Carrolls' Castle was being enacted, the lads that left our kitchen had gone and removed the pike heads from the gardens in the village and transported them up to Glenleitir Valley, where they put them in a safe hiding place.

When I was a young lad and I went up into the valley, I was shown where Jimmy Ryan's complement of pikes were buried above in the mountain.

Actually they did dig the hole at the castle that night. My father, he brought me over when I was young and he told me the story, he said they dug the hole, so the police would know they were there. And you know what? That hole is still there![21]

*A pike is a weapon consisting of a long pole with a steel or iron shaft on top. Under the spear point was a sharpened blade with which to cut the reins of a horseman. Pikes were constructed locally, made covertly by blacksmiths and craftspeople in preparation for the rebellions of 1687 and 1798.

Animal Lore from the Mountain

People who lived in the Slieve Blooms were very fond of animals. Their whole lives revolved around the world of nature and much of their stories and folklore are built around animal tales. Place names remind us of animals which have long since disappeared from the landscape. The Wolftrap Mountain, south of the village of Cadamstown, reminds us that the wolf inhabited the island for thousands of years. The ring forts, which were the first dwelling places for farmers, were surrounded by earthen ramparts to protect the inhabitants and the animals from marauding wolves. The early Christian monasteries had earthen enclosures for protection against wild animals, such as wolves.

The old people had good stories to tell about wolves. In the area around Wolftrap Mountain they could show you where pits were dug to trap the animals. There was once a farmer in another part of the country who dug a pit and covered it with branches to trap a wolf. On the following day they discovered a wolf, a woman and a monk in the pit. All friends, no doubt!

Hens

In ancient Irish manuscripts a laying hen was valued at two bushels of grain, whereas a cock was valued at one bushel. A goose egg was more prized than a hen egg.

Folk tradition is rich with stories about eggs. They were marked with crosses to bring good luck. When a hen began to hatch, a horseshoe was placed under the nest. Rotten eggs were placed in haystacks to bring bad luck to the household. A crowing hen was unlucky and was not left alive for long. The crowing of a cock was believed to be effective against spirits.

The cock crowing three times has not only a powerful meaning in the Bible, as in foretelling the tragic events to come, but the course of many stories change when the cock crows.

The March cock has certain powers but has to be black in colour. Local folklore tells that the Danes brought hens to Ireland. So hens continue to harbour hostile feelings towards the Irish;

their scratchings on the floor of the kitchen are supposedly a vain attempt to set the house on fire!

Bees

Almost every house in the Slieve Bloom Mountains kept a hive of bees. Honey was a cure for sore throats and was used to flavour drinks and herbal remedies. A drink made with heather blossoms mixed with honey was a special treat. If a bee entered a house through a door or window, it was good luck. It was also good luck if the bee settled in the thatch of a house. If it came down the chimney, a calamity would occur. If bees left, bad luck would follow. It was customary when a member of the family died to leave a piece of black cloth on the hive so that the bees could join in the mourning.

Applying a sliced onion or a ball of blue or the water which lay in a cow dung was thought to cure the sting of a bee.

In my young days, when sitting by the big open fire, especially in harvest time, a large bee would descend. We called it a 'hurley-buz'. We loved to see this creature. It would announce its presence

by emitting a noise like an aeroplane. We were told not to harm it. We would open all doors and windows so that it could return to its natural habitat.

The Salmon, the Eel and the Otter

Living by the banks of the Silver River, we were familiar with the coming of the salmon. We loved to watch him in the depths of the pools; we knew when he had arrived by the small ridges in the sandbanks in the bed of the river. During the night, the hen salmon laid her eggs and the cock fertilised them and covered

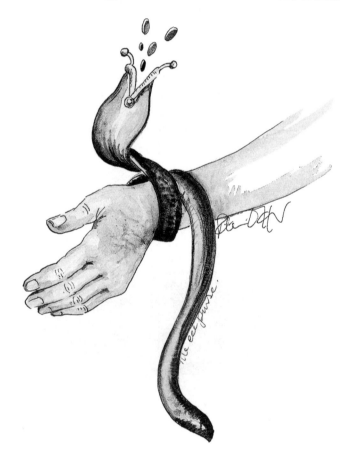

them with his tail. The story was that a salmon that inhabited the *poll doimhne* (the deep pool) was a magic fish that could never be caught. According to tradition, if you could just see him, your wish would be granted, no matter what it was.

The eel also had special powers. He could travel miles overland at night so a purse made of an eel skin would never be empty. If anyone suffered from a sprained wrist, called a '*trálach*', the practice was to put a band from an eel skin around the affected part. There is a legend about an eel that was caught at the *cuan* on the Silver River. The woman of the house was preparing to cook it when the eel spoke up and said, '*Amach leat*' (out with you). The woman opened the door and released the eel.

Now that the fish have left our rivers, the otter has become very scarce. In the mountain areas, the otter was known as the *madra uisce* (water dog). There is a story about a family who were suffering great hunger during the famine times and were kept alive by their pet otter.

The king otter always sleeps with his eyes open. It was customary to keep an otter's skin in the house as it would protect the house against fire. When people emigrated from the mountain, they would bring a piece of otter skin with them for good luck.

Badgers and Rabbits

The badger (*an broc*) was well respected and many places owe their names to him. He saves hay for the farmers by turning *somaháns* (grass cocks) at night, looking for slugs. He is not a good runner and, when pursued by dogs, he is said to catch his tail in his mouth and roll downhill.

The rabbits were brought in by the Normans. A pot of rabbit soup was a cure for illness because rabbits live on herbs.

Hedgehogs

Hedgehogs, or *gráinneoga*, were once a common sight in woodlands. They are welcomed by gardeners as they eat slugs and other vermin. It is said that they suck milk from the cows when they are lying down.

The Hare

The hare is looked upon as supernatural. It is bad luck if he crosses the path of a pregnant woman.

The stories of old women (or witches) turning into hares are numerous on and around the mountains.

Rats

Rats were thought to bring bad luck.

Birds

The ancient Druids held birds in great reverence.

A hooded crow around the house was said to be an ill omen. The magpie is still thought to bring bad luck; always remove your hat when you see one.

The robin used to be held in high regard. It was advisable never to molest a robin's nest. It was said that the robin followed certain families and when a family member died it sang on the windowsill.

Frogs

It was lucky to see a frog on the door step. You had to lick him to cure certain ailments.

Spider

The spider brought good luck. You were never to kill a spider; if you did, it would bring you bad luck.

Crows

Crows building nests around the house brought good luck. If they left, the family would soon die out. The weather was judged by the antics of the crows: if they stayed around the farmhouse during the day, bad weather was imminent; if they grew noisy, a storm was approaching.

They were thought to start building their nests as near as possible to 1 March.

There is a story that a crow invited a wren to show him how to build his nest. Every twig the wren placed on the nest, the crow would say, 'I know that'. The wren became enraged and said, 'Since you know so much now finish your nest'.

That is why the crow is such a bad builder and maybe there is a moral in the story for all of us.

31

TALES FROM NEILSTOWN

Paddy Dooley is from Neilstown, which used to be called Baile Laidhreach, meaning the 'forked pass'. It was an important pass in ancient times since the old road between Leinster and Munster passed along it.

Paddy told me a number of stories about Neilstown, some very ancient and some in living memory. This one took place during the War of Independence.

BINOCULARS IN THE WASHTUB

There was a raid one time on Roundwood House, which is now a guesthouse and an upmarket restaurant. It was carried out by the local IRA brigade. They were looking for guns and arms, but they got other things as well, including a pair of binoculars.

A local man, whose name I won't mention, was one of the volunteers and he came down to the house we're in now to show it to my grandfather and grandmother. It was something to see, a rare enough object in those times. My grandmother was working away at the window, doing the washing, as usual. It would have been done with a basin and washtub in those days. She stopped what she was doing to examine the binoculars when they heard engines coming into the yard. It was the RIC and the auxiliaries coming to search the place.

The young volunteer went as white as a sheet, but my grandfather leapt up, grabbed the binoculars and threw them into the washtub. My grandmother continued washing away.

The RIC came in and searched the house from top to bottom, but they never saw the binoculars in washtub. That's the story, and it's a true one!

THE O'NEILLS

Neilstown got its name from the number of families of the name O'Neill that lived there at one time. Before that it was called Baile

Laidhreach. The story was that the army of Hugh O'Neill and O'Donnell passed along the way to face the British forces at the Battle of Kinsale in 1688. They camped south of Borris-in-Ossory on Sentry Hill, as it's now called.

After the defeat at the Battle of Kinsale, the stragglers passed along the way again, but this time they stayed. They had nothing to go back to in Tyrone as their leaders, the last of the Gaelic chieftains, would in time take flight for Europe. Tradition has it that the demoralised followers walked into houses that were empty, took them over and eventually married locally. Between Neilstown and Cadamstown and Kinnitty on the Offaly side of the Slieve Blooms, you come across a lot of northern names, like Heaney, Donnelly, McGuinness and Corrigan. People were given the name O'Neill if they were followers of the Great O'Neill, as Hugh O'Neill, the chieftain of the clan, was called.

They cut down forests and cultivated lands and became small farmholders in the area. The last family of O'Neills who lived in Neilstown were proud of the fact that they were descendants of O'Neill of Tyrone. They felt they were part of the aristocracy. They had worked hard and endured hardship, but they were proud of their ancestry.

THE *LIOS* OF THE OLD WOMAN OF LEINSTER

Not far from the crossroads, just down the hill where the Dooley family live, you come across a sign which says, '*Lios*'. A *lios* is the Irish word for a fort, often a fort that is thought to be the domain of the fairies. This particular *lios*, which is covered in a mossy tangle of trees and bushes, is just off the roadway and has an eerie, unsettling feel about it. It is possessed of an atmosphere that says, 'Keep out!' It is named in the Book of Leinster, a twelfth-century manuscript, as '*Lios na gCailigh Laighnigh*', the *lios* of the Old Woman of Leinster.

There was another *lios*, about a mile away, on the Offaly side of the mountain, called *Lios na gCailigh Mumhnaigh*, the *lios* of the Old Woman of Munster. In ancient times, the crossroads marked a provincial boundary. The Offaly territory would have been Ely O'Carroll territory, which was Munster territory. There is little trace of the *lios* on the Munster side now, but it was an important place in the olden times. It was known as a *bruíon*, or a hostel. People travelling from Leinster to Munster would stay overnight in that *lios* and then travel on the following day.

It was harvest time and the old woman of the *lios* of Leinster was paying off the labourers for their work. The payment was a loaf of bread for each labourer. She was a shrewd, watchful woman and one particular lad came up to her whom she didn't recognise. She said to him, 'You haven't been working with the others; you are not entitled to a loaf of bread.'

'Do you know who I am?' he replied.

'I don't,' she said.

'I am a messenger from the king of Munster and if I don't get my loaf of bread, I'll bring the warriors of Munster up here and they will lay this place bare.' But that didn't frighten the old *cailleach* of Leinster.

'Right,' she said, 'bring them on, but if you do, I'll call on the warriors of Leinster and they'll show your warriors a thing or two.' The insults continued on in that way until one or other gave in. So that will tell you what an important place *Lios na gCailligh Laignigh* was in ancient times.

Another story from Paddy Dooley tells of his great-grandmother, who was a Ryan from Drumbane in Upperchurch, which is situated in County Tipperary, between Thurles and Cashel. How she came to marry into a family so far away up in the mountain is not known. But the suspicion was that Paddy's great-grandfather met her when they were selling firkins of butter at the butter market in Thurles. That's how the connection was made. She married his great-grandfather up there in 1862. She was a native Irish speaker because the Irish language was still alive in the Upperchurch Drumbane area.

The story goes that one day a little man appeared in her kitchen. Naturally she was terrified, but he said he wasn't going to harm her in any way, but that he had come over from the fairy fort and he wanted to warn her that she would hear very bad news within the next day or two. Then he disappeared. Within a day or two, she got word that her brother had been killed. He either fell off a horse or got a kick of a horse, but he died anyway. That's a story that's come down in the family from the fort.

Some people talk about the *cailleach* of the *lios* as a hag, but Paddy prefers to call her the Old Woman of Leinster and believes she was respected as well as feared by the people of Neilstown. As children, they were warned to keep away from the *lios*. Coming up to Christmas, people would collect holly. There was always plenty of holly up at the fort, but even if holly was scarce everywhere else nobody from the area would go into the *lios* to get the holly under any circumstances.

In the summertime, Paddy remembers his grand-uncle Pierce telling him about the fairy blasts that would come up the road in hot weather. A fairy blast was a mini tornado of dust, which would sweep along the road. You would hear it coming; the leaves would start fluttering on the trees. His uncle told him it was a fairy funeral and that the fairies were burying one of their own. One hot summer's day, the men were making hay in the field and the fairy blast came down the road. They had a little terrier with them. The little dog heard the whish of the wind coming down the road, and ran out and got caught up in the mini tornado. It turned and went into the *lios* and, according to Paddy's uncle, the dog was never seen again. Is it any wonder the children stayed out of the *lios*?

The reason the *lios* is still there today, and in such a good state, is that people were terrified to interfere with it. 'The landowner there now would not touch that *lios* in a thousand years. The hill out there was always known as Lios Hill. We always used to say, "Leave the fort to the fairies. If you do interfere with it, bad luck will surely follow you."'

STORIES OF THE FAMINE

Down the road from the Dooleys' house is what is known as a famine road. It was built during the famine as a relief road. The workers

were paid a penny a day. It's really a road to nowhere, but they weren't going to give the workers money for nothing, so they built the road for a penny a day.

There is very little folklore or stories about the famine in this area. Paddy's opinion is that there were no survivors and those who did survive lived with a sense of guilt. His mother told him that during the famine their family, who had a fair-sized farm up near the county boundary, would stay up at night with shotguns to guard the potatoes in case somebody came along and stole them. It was a case of survival of the fittest. That's not the kind of thing people would be too proud of.

The cottier population all disappeared and it was the relatively strong tenant farmers who survived. The Dooleys walked into their house and took it over. The people who lived there before were named Palmers. They were Protestants, but they couldn't pay the rent, so they had to go. They disappeared overnight. This explodes the myth that it was only Catholics who were evicted. If you were Protestant and couldn't pay, you still had to go. There was an expression locally, 'Ah sure, they walked into it', meaning that many a family moved into a house from which the previous tenants had been evicted.

MAGGIE NEILL

There was once a great old woman called Maggie Neill, who used to tell stories. Paddy and his friends used to go down to listen to her. She would close her eyes and she wouldn't open them for hours as she told the stories. The stories related what happened in her young days around the area. They were never written down but she was brilliant and when Paddy was about ten to fourteen, there wasn't much to do, so listening to Maggie was a great pastime. A lot of the stories were snippets about things that had happened in her young days.

She used to tell one story about the time of Parnell. There were Parnellites and Anti-Parnellites.

There was great division in the country at that time. It was nearly as bad as the division during the civil war. In Camross, there was a cricket team. It was an anti-Parnellite cricket team. They arranged a match between another team from Laois who were Parnellites. The team came to Camross and they were all set up for this cricket match. There was a priest in Camross at that time. He came out. He put down a crucifix between the two wickets and defied anybody to bowl a ball across the crucifix because he was so opposed to them playing a team which supported Parnell. That was a story Maggie Neill told.

North Tipperary, just over the county boundary was a very active place during the War of Independence. Four hundred years ago an army of thousands, the army of O'Neill and O'Donnell, passed along the road on the way on the way to Kinsale and they were utterly defeated.

On 11 July 1921, the men of the North Tipperary Flying Column marched up this road to camp at Doire Leathan. There would have been no more than thirty or forty of them. Paddy Dooley reflected on the army of thousands, which was utterly defeated, and those few men who went on to set up the state we live in today.[22]

32

THE TALES OF DAN CULLETON

Of all the people I met in the Slieve Bloom area during the time I spent there, Dan was the closest to what most people in Ireland understand as a seanchaí. He had the local lore and stories, along with a love of entertaining an audience. He would begin to talk about some local event or custom and in no time at all, he would spin you a yarn that would leave you in stitches.

Camross is in north Laois. It extends up to the top of the Slieve Bloom Mountains and on the other side is Kinnitty, which is in County Offaly. Dan was born and reared in Glendine Lane, which goes up to the famous Gap of Glendine. He worked on the small farm he grew up on and has rich memories of the stares (the starlings) in wintertime. They would nestle there up in the gap and at about four o'clock in the evening, a big black cloud of stares would begin to wheel and a hawk would be waiting for them and the big black cloud would break up and spread out. It was a remarkable sight, which has always stood out in his memory.

THE GAP OF GLENDINE

There was supposed to be a spirit laid at the Gap of Glendine in the form of a dog in a barrel down at the Knockanad Road. A priest in

Camross was supposed to have laid him there for eighty years. I think he should be released soon. He's been up there as long as I remember.

BANSHEES

Most of the stories that I remember in this area were about spirits. Banshees and spirits and dogs and their gullets. The banshee (*bean sí*); a little small woman combing her hair, and all that. There were old fellas used to ramble at our house at a time and one story would be better than another, or worse than another, if you like! They'd be telling a spirit that was up the road, or down the road, or about meeting the banshee and listening to the banshee.

Now I never heard a banshee, but I was with fellas who said they did. I remember I was with a fella coming home at night from rambling[23] and there was seven or eight of us. And the fella I was with turned to me and he said, 'My grandmother must be going to die.'

I said to him, 'How is that?'

He says, 'I can hear the banshee. Can you hear her?'

But I couldn't hear her.

There was another fella and I always believed him. He said he met the banshee. He was going through the middle of a field where there was a path and he was taking a shortcut home. He heard her first and then in a split second, he had to step off the path to let her pass.

Rory Oy.

'What was she?' I asked.

'She was a small little woman with grey hair, or fair hair. I couldn't tell which.'

'Were you frightened?'

'I wasn't.'

I was coming home one night from a wake. It was about four o'clock in the morning. I was just after leaving school and the wakes at that time would go on all night. There were pipes and tobacco at the wakes and you'd nearly sicken yourself at them. The fella that was with me going home, a next-door neighbour, he says, 'Stand for a minute.' We stood. The banshee used to follow this fella I was with. 'Can you hear her?' he'd say.

'I can't,' says I.

'Ah God,' he says, 'she's up agin us there.'

I couldn't hear anything.

THE BLACK DOG

This is a story that happened in the parish. There was potato-picking going on in the place. There was a Church of Ireland man and he hadn't been going to church. There were a lot of Catholics of course there too and they saw the Protestant minister coming and the Church of Ireland man said, 'Don't say that I'm here.' There was big kish, or a skip, and the Catholic man says to him, 'Get in there, under the kish. I'll put the top over on you, and he won't see you.' So in came the minister and he began to enquire about the man. He was looking for him. The other man walked over to the kish and he lifted the top off. 'There he is,' he said. The Protestant was mortified when the top was taken off the kish and the minister there looking at him. So he said to the Catholic man, 'I'll get you, dead or alive!'

The Church of Ireland man died some time after. After a short time the Catholic man and another man were coming from rambling and a black dog leapt up on your man's back. He followed him up the road and when they got to the crossroads where they were going to separate, the man said, 'I can't go home. This dog is after me

Banshee

and I know who he is.' They stopped and the dog leapt up on him and he threw him down on the road. The neighbour invited him back to his own house for the night, where he thought he'd be safe.

The next morning they got up and the dog was dead!

RABBITS AND THE CURE

We had a small farm of about twenty-five acres. I was the eldest boy. When I left school I had to work the farm. I had a brother and three sisters. One of my sisters died when she was 11 years old. My mother died very young too. They were hard times, the thirties and early forties. You had the economic war and the Second World War and there was no jobs and all that.

But I'll tell you what was a great money-spinner at the time: rabbits. Ireland was crawling with rabbits at the time and during the war, I can remember, the rabbits made four shillings. If you were working with a farmer and had a pound a week at that time, you would think you were doing very well. If you could catch five rabbits in the week and nothing else, you'd still have a pound. The local shops would buy the rabbits at whatever was the going rate at the time and they'd take them to Dublin and the people there would buy the rabbits.

There were four or five ways of catching rabbits at the time: you could trap him or snare him or hunt him with dogs, or you could ferret him. The ferret came from the family of the weasel. You'd put the ferret into the burrow or the ditch. You'd hear the noise inside when the ferret caught the rabbit and you'd probably have to dig him out. You'd have a bar and a spade, and you'd put down the bar to see where the rabbit was and you would dig him out.

Myxomatosis came to Ireland in 1954 and it finished the rabbits. Most of the young lads were hunting after the rabbits in the wintertime. During the summer, they'd have jobs on the bogs or different jobs with farmers and when winter would come they would be back with the rabbits again. But myxomatosis put an end to it all. The rabbits' heads would swell up and they would be going around stupid, running into the walls and all that. The myx-omatosis was brought in because the rabbits were breeding too fast and doing damage to the crops. They were pests.

Anyway, most of the young lads went to England at that time. There wasn't enough work here to keep them going.

There was this fella – Jack was his name – and he went over to England. He started working on the buildings over there as there was no job here for him.

So after about six months' hard work, he wasn't feeling so well, so he decided to go to the doctor and see if here was anything wrong with him. The doctor examined him, but could find nothing wrong at all. 'I'll tell you,' says the doctor. 'I'll give you these pills and they'll help you. You'll feel so well, you'll look 30 years of age.'

'But Doctor,' said Jack, 'I'm only 25!'

'Take them home,' said the doctor. 'You'll want them some time.'

So Jack took the pills home and thought about it. He thought about his mother at home doing all the work and he decided she would need the pills more than he did. So he sent home the pills and thought no more about them.

After a year or so, he decided he'd come home and visit his mother and father and see how they were getting on. He was walking up through the village and going down the far side was this magnificent blonde woman wheeling a pram and a good lump of a child in it. And she stood and called over to him, 'Well, hello, Jack, you never told us you were coming home!' Jack stood and looked across at this lovely blonde woman.

'Excuse me now,' he says. 'You have me now. I'm not away too long, but I don't know you?'

'Ah, Jack,' she says, 'Don't tell me now, but do you not know your own mother?'

'You're my mother!' says Jack. 'In the name of God, what did you do with yourself?'

'Well,' she said, 'I took one of the pills that you sent home for me.'

'And who's that child in the pram?'

'That's your father,' she said. 'He got the other two!'[24]

33

THE TALES OF MICK DOWLING

Mick Dowling was born in Derry, or Derrycarew, in the Slieve Bloom Mountains. He had a great interest in history and folklore from an early age, mainly, he believed, because he spent a lot of time in his youth with his grandmother. His grandmother, he said, was the outdoor type. Her husband died when her children were very young. Mick's father was one of the oldest and he was only seven at the time. As a result, she had to work both inside and outside the house.

'My grandmother was about five foot in height and she was broad-shouldered and very sturdy. That was her appearance and her mind worked the same way. If she met the bull in a field, it would be the bull would step back, not her. My grandmother moved down from Gleann Kitt in the Slieve Blooms to Derrycarew. In a lot of houses there might have been two women in the house and they mightn't have got on. My grandmother would have been the outdoor type and so when I was knocking around, she was mostly doing the outside work.'

Mick's great-grandfather was executed after the 1798 Rebellion for a raid he carried out on Capard House. His grandmother was one of the last Irish speakers in the area and he remembers being taught only through the medium of Irish in school.

Granny

GREGORY COSTIGAN, THE OUTLAW

Gleann Cit, where Mick Dowling's grandparents came from, was beside an area in the mountains called Gort na gCloch, meaning the field of stones.

At one time there were thirty-two families living there. They grew corn, turnips and potatoes. Most of the corn was used to make illicit *poíteen*, and the rest was fed to the animals. On one Christmas Eve, in the black year of 1847, thirteen of those families were evicted and their shacks were burned down, one of them being the shelter for a mother and son by the name of Costigan.

There was also an area of very good land in the centre of the mountain, called the Islands, which was controlled by the Ascendancy. Foremost among the planters at the time was Sir Charles Coote, who lived with his family in a mansion called Rushall Court. The lands around the Pike of Rushall used to belong to the MacCostigans, who were a powerful Gaelic family in the area. Their lands were confiscated in Cromwellian times and the younger members of the MacCostigans clan, four brothers who failed in the courts to get their lands back, were forced to turn rapparees[25] and take to the glens and bogs of the Slieve Bloom Mountains.

Mick told me the story of Gregory Costigan, the eldest of the brothers, who remained at large long after the others had been captured and executed. There was a price on Gregory's head, but he had managed to evade capture for a long time. He was protected by local people and would repay them by stealing a cow for them from one of the landed gentry. He was eventually betrayed by one of his own relatives, his own nephew, the child of his sister, a man called Sean Gearr.

Gregory, it is said, was drinking one night in a shebeen in Glenconra, run by an old woman. There were soldiers present and Gregory, after a few drinks, wanting more, offered one to the woman of the house. She, in an attempt to warn him of the danger replied, '*Ól féin é, daor an deoch duit é* (Drink it yourself, it will cost you a lot). Gregory didn't take the hint and later went off and made his way back to *Gort na gCloch*.

He travelled from Glencondra into Carrowree and there in a boggy hollow he was confronted and surrounded there by the red-coats and his betrayer, Sean Gearr. He was beheaded on a stone on the south-eastern corner of Gort na gCloch. The stone is there to this day. Mick brought me to the spot and showed me the conglomerate sandstone standing almost two-feet high where Gregory, the last of the Costigans, bled to death.

His bloodstained head was carried on the point of a spear to the Cootes' house at Rushall. The wife of one of the Coote family came to the door and is said to have fainted when the head of Gregory Costigan, still impaled on the spear, was produced from the bag. She later lost the child she was carrying. Shortly afterwards she returned to England and cut all connections with the

Coote family, whom she regarded as more barbarous than any of the Irish she was surrounded by.

Sean Gearr was taken by the local people back up to Glenann Mountain, on the edge of Gleann Cit, where there was a track about a foot wide, dug down into the bog. He was taken and forced head first down into the bog. They didn't kill him, but they left him with the blood running into his head to think it over before he died.[26]

A version of this story was also collected by Br. Dan Hassett f.s.c in a collection of folklore from Laois printed in 1985.

34

THE TALES OF
JENNY MCGLYNN

*Jenny McGlynn (née Dunne) lived in Mountmellick, County Laois,
all her life. She told me about the rambling houses in the bay area
where she lived after she was married to Tom McGlynn, and the cottages in Manor Land, where she grew up, as Jane Dunne, and where
stories of ghosts and the little people and the other world were part
and parcel of her life.*

*Jenny is the only person I met in Laois who claims to have seen the
banshee.*

I saw the banshee in the yard the night my mother died. My mother
was dying and I was minding her. I thought I heard the gate
opening. I was expecting my brothers home. I had let them go out
for a pint. When I heard the noise I opened the door and looked
out. As soon as I opened the door this white figure came right at
me, she almost got to me and then went across the yard.

She was small and dressed all in white. I couldn't make out a
face, just dark holes where the eyes should be. Of course I stiffened
with fear. I wasn't able to take in a lot.

Of course I bolted the door and I went back into Mammy's
room and I sat down on the bed with her and didn't leave until my
brothers got back.

That was on a Saturday night.

On Sunday morning my neighbour came in. Her name was Mrs Fitzgerald, God rest her. She said, 'Did you hear herself last night, under your mother's window? She was roaring the place down.'

I heard nothing, never heard a sound.

About seven o'clock on Sunday evening, Mammy took a bad turn and within an hour, she was dead. It didn't register with me straight off it was the banshee I saw, but I knew then that it was her.

There would have been a lot of noises heard on Manor Lane, where I grew up. We were the middle house on the lane. You'd hear men marching and strange lights coming out from among the trees.

Not glow-worms. Lights. Like a ball of fire. The banshee is supposed to walk the lane at night. In those days, it used to be pitch dark. There are a few lights there now. I was never afraid going up in the dark. Never afraid.

But I'd never be out during the dead hours, between twelve o'clock at night and three in the morning. I'd either be home before twelve or wait until after three. Those are the hours where you leave the dead to go about and you don't want to be in their way.

I believe there are evil spirits as well as good spirits still on the land. I do believe it.

My father used to work on a farm. He used to come down a laneway about half a mile long. He was due to be home at half past six, but he was delayed. He was coming down the lane at five past twelve when the bike was pulled from under him. He couldn't cycle it and it was held solid. It was only released at three o'clock after he had been pulling away, wondering what was holding it.

When he came into the light of the house, he fainted out cold. I remember that well. He was a strong man, my father.

Night-Time Encounters

There was another man who used to drink a lot. He lived up the lane.

At that time there was a little river with no wall. You could fall into it easily. His mother came out looking for him one night.

He was lying on the bank of the river with his hand out, saying, 'Give me your hand and I'll pull you out!' The mother had a habit of carrying holy water with her and she sprinkled the water on her son to get the devil away from him. A blue light came up from the river. The man sobered up and walked home with his mother.

My husband Tom was a great storyteller. He told all kinds of stories. He used to work at Bórd na Móna and one night when he was coming home in the dark from working a night shift, he saw lights on the bog. Thinking they were the lights of the town, he followed them. But he realised he was going the wrong way. He then changed direction, but that was the wrong way too. Then he realised the only way to get out of it was to take off his coat and turn it inside out. He continued to wear it that way until he got back on a track. He did come home with his coat inside out. I was waiting up for him to give him his supper.

I thought he'd been to the pub, but he hadn't.

Some of the stories I heard were old wives' tales, but some were true. I do believe in spirits, I do. You have to believe in spirits. If you didn't, you couldn't believe in God. That's my belief anyway.

Some people are born to see things and others can't. My own daughter could see, from the time she was a baby. We'd be coming down the road in the dark and she'd pull me out into the light. She would have seen this particular man. My mother then told me that there was a man who used to live around that spot and he was supposed to have sworn that he would stay on his land, dead or alive. My daughter could see him, but I couldn't.

The Rusheen

The fairy rath we had up the bog lane was called the Rusheen. But it was burnt down. The man who burned it down had no luck afterwards. The poor unfortunate chap was deranged and he hung himself after. He hung himself and was saved, then a couple of years later, he poisoned himself.

People weren't afraid of the rath at all. As long as you didn't take anything out of it, you'd never have any harm befall you. But if you took a stick out of it, anything could happen. My father-in-law used to tell this story.

THE TREE AND THE WHIP

'A man cut a branch off a sally tree to herd his cattle. He didn't think twice about it and he was herding them out on to the road. When a little man came up and handed him a cow's tale and said, "There's a whip for your stick!"

'The Rusheen was a gorgeous and peaceful place. There was a centrepiece; it was soft like velvet and there'd be a ring of daisies all around. And a little tree, like a chair, with a cushion of moss in the fork. There were three branches coming out of this cushion. I often sat on it when I was a child and we'd be there playing. And as an adult, when Tom and I would go walking, we used to go around it. We always went to that same spot. It was a lovely place to be. No matter how windy it was out along the bog, when you'd go there, it would be warm. There wouldn't be even a breeze through the trees.

'And you could hear music. I often heard music. I often looked around to see if there was anyone playing or if there was someone with a radio. It was Irish music. You couldn't make it out, whether it was one instrument or more. The music was just there, but you couldn't make it out. We didn't ever use the word 'fairy'. It was the 'little people'.

If you didn't cross them, they wouldn't cross you. You respect them, they'll respect you. Do harm on them and they will do harm on you.

A bride would have to wear a patch of red with a darning needle on it so she wouldn't be taken. Because the fairies had no blood, not like the human race. If they saw blood, they'd run away. They don't have any blood, so they don't die. They won't go to heaven.

The same with a baby. My mother-in-law used to say, if the child got too cross, 'That's a changeling'. So they would put something red near the child to protect it. I don't remember that in my family, but my mother-in-law used to say, 'That one's taken'. I think she really believed in it, she did!

The little people never cursed or swore and to change the child back, they used terrible language in the room where the child was. They didn't curse or swear at the child, they just used bad language in the room where the child was. I can't use that language, but they'd be effin' and blindin' and eventually the child would quieten down. It would terrify a child. Wouldn't it? Even at my age, if I hear an argument and bad language, I get into the corner, and I'd be terrified!

There was an old lady, used to live in Manor Road. She was very old and we used to call into her on the way home from school to get her water or go down for bread for her. Some days we'd go in and she'd say, 'Shh, don't stir, they're dancing there on the hearth.'

You see the ashes would be spinning there on the hearth. You'd see them spinnin' around, like the whirlwinds you'd see on television. She'd be sitting there watching them dancing. We could see the white ashes from the turf and we were innocent enough to believe her.[27]

35

DAVID
NORRIS

David Norris is an independent senator in Dáil Éireann. He is also a civil and human rights activist, a Joycean scholar and a proud son of Laois.

This very popular and energetic man was born in Africa, but at the age of six months was brought back by his parents to Ireland. The family went straight to the home of his maternal grandfather near Mountrath, close to the Slieve Bloom Mountains.

He always considered Laois to be 'home', although his parents subsequently moved to Dublin, where he was educated.

His mother's family, the Fitzpatricks, could trace their ancestry right back to the time when the clan of Mac Giolla Phádraig (the Fitzpatricks) were the dominant tribe in Laois and held the title of kings of Ossory.

According to David, the Fitzpatricks originally controlled all of Laois, a lot of Kilkenny and even some of Waterford, right out to the sea.

'But we were put in our box by the arrival of the Butlers, the Dukes of Ormonde in Kilkenny. They even stole our title, the Earls of Ossory – they grabbed that and we were squished up to be Earls of Upper Ossory.

'In fact when I arranged a birthday party to celebrate my aunt's ninetieth birthday, the menus and invitations were printed up "To Celebrate the 90th Birthday of the Countess of Upperossity!"

'My aunt was only half interested in her ancestral connections with royalty, but my grandfather used to say, Someone who puts sixpence in my pocket was of more use to me!'

David Norris's family in Laois, he says, were people with a great sense of humour and life. His beloved aunt lived to be 103. A distant cousin, who lived in Key West in Florida, lived to be 105.

David's boyhood was spent travelling to Laois on the Limerick bus to visit his Mountmellick cousins. 'I always knew when I was nearing home. I could smell the peat. I love Laois and the Slieve Blooms and the piercing champagne-like air. My favourite paintings are of boggy landscapes, dull leaden skies and still water.'

The family were great talkers and they would talk about people who were in the First World War. Those became as real to him as the people who walked the street every day. He remembers the Big Wheeler, who had a tuneless voice and who was always a line or two behind everyone else singing hymns in church. There was also an employee of his grandfather who got married. 'My grandfather asked her when she came home from the honeymoon how was married life. She said, "Mister Fitzpatrick, I love him surely. Every fart he lets out is like a new laid egg to me!"'

Another lady gave birth to a son and she was looking around for a grand name for him, so she called her son John Joseph Francis Elastic Paul Albert!

'My uncle used to cut turf in the Slieve Bloom Mountains and used to tell me stories when I was small about leprechauns who lived up there. They lived in places with wonderful names such as Ballyhuppahane. Where else would leprechauns live except in Ballyhuppahane in the Slieve Bloom Mountains? They were cunning and wily creatures who made the most beautiful shoes and who had a purse of gold sovereigns. I could see them, they were all in my mind.'

There were many stories of eccentric ancestors in David Norris's family.

'One of our relations in the eighteenth century had a nagging wife and at long last, she died. They lived in a rambling old house and they were carrying the coffin down the back stairs and it banged off the corner of the wall. The next thing there was a tapping on the coffin and they opened it up and there she was, alive! She lived for another ten years and gave him hell.

'Eventually she died and as they were coming down the staircase, her husband said, "Mind that corner boy!"'

'She must have been in a catatonic coma the first time around.'

Another of his ancestors, also in the eighteenth century, married an heiress from England. She was more or less disinherited for marrying this fellow, who was a gambler.

On her deathbed, she made him swear that he wouldn't sell her bed. But then things became difficult again and he did sell it on.

The neighbours bought it. Next thing, there were new carriages and furniture and all kinds of improvements in the house next door.

The bed had been stuffed with gold sovereigns.

The Senator and his Aunt

I asked David to tell me the story concerning himself and his aunt which had been doing the rounds in County Laois and which I'd heard a number of times. Here it is in his own words.

My aunt and uncle and I were staying at Roundwood House, a couple of miles outside Mountrath, on the way to the Slieve Bloom Mountains.

It was built by an ancestor of mine, a Quaker by the name of Sharpe. Roundwood House is now a very good guesthouse, which specialises in excellent food and hospitality. I took my aunt, who was elderly, for a drive in the mountains. We went across the Cut and then around by Rosenallis and we came to a demesne wall and my aunt said, 'Oh, that's Capard House. We used to play cards there in the 1920s.'

I assumed that it was now the same kind of operation as Roundwood House so I said, 'We'll call in for a cup of tea.' So we sailed up the drive, and there were only two cars parked outside. I thought, oh, the poor things, we'd better eat our heads off and support local industry. We banged on the door and a woman came out and said, 'Can I help you?'

And I said, 'Yes, thank you, we'd like some afternoon tea.'

She said, 'Certainly, sir, where would you like it? On the steps, in the drawing room or in the library?'

'Oh,' I said. 'It's a lovely evening. Why not let us stay out on the steps and enjoy the wonderful view and the balmy air?'

'She said, 'Certainly, what would you like?'

I said, 'Tea, homemade scones if you have them. Some brown bread, some homemade jam if you have it. That would be lovely.'

She said, 'Certainly, sir.' Then she brought out the tea. It was lovely, everything was grand. We thoroughly enjoyed it.

After about a half an hour she came back and said, 'How was that? Can I get you anything else, sir?'

And I said, 'No, thank you, that was grand, just the bill.'

'The bill?' she said. 'Oh, but this is a private house!'

It's exactly the same plot as in the play *She Stoops to Conquer* by Richard Brindsley Sheridan, but it's true![28]

NOTES

1. Vincent Woods, *Folklore and Modern Irish Writing*, Eds Anne O'Connor and Anne Markey (Irish Academic Press, 2014).
2. NFC:36.
3. Laois Oral Archive, CD.1.
4. NFC:36:61-62.
5. NFC.36:185.
6. ibid.
7. Laois Oral Archive, CD.1.
8. ibid.
9. ibid.
10. Laois Oral Archive, CD.6.
11. NFC:36:221-230.
12. NFC:127:334-436. Collected by Seosaimhín Céitinn.
13. NFC:25-36.
14. NFC:36:1-15.
15. NFC:36:269-272.
16. Laois Oral Archive, CD.6.
17. NFC:36:133-134.
18. NFCS. James Quigley, 87 years. Collected by Robert O'Byrne, NT, Timahoe.
19. ibid.
20. ibid.
21. Laois Oral Archive, CD.7.

22. Laois Oral Archive, CD.4.
23. Rambling – 'Night visiting from house to house for gossip and entertainment' (Terry Dolan. Hiberno-English dictionary).
24. Laois Oral Archive, CD.2.
25. A 'rapparee' is an outlaw or highwayman.
26. Laois Oral Archive, CD.5.
27. Laois Oral Archive, CD.9.
28. Recorded 27 February 2015 by N.H.

FURTHER READING

BOOKS AND ARTICLES

J. Feehan, *Laois: an Environmental History* (Ballykilcavan Press; Stradbally, 1984)

J. Feehan, *The Landscape of Slieve Bloom: A Study of its Natural and Human Heritage* (Blackwater Press; Dublin, 1979)

Paddy Heaney, *At the foot of Slieve Bloom: History and Folklore of Cadamstown*, published by Kilcormac Historical Society

John Keegan, *Selected Works*, edited by Tony Delaney (Galmoy Press, 1997)

P. Lane & Nolan W., *Laois, History and Society* (Geography Publications; Dublin, 1999)

Lageniensis (John Canon O'Hanlon), *Local Legends of Ireland Folklore and Legends of Ireland*

Anne O'Connor and Anne Markey (eds), *Folklore and Modern Irish Writing* (Irish Academic Press, 1915)

Revd John Canon O'Hanlon, A *History of the Queens County* (1908)

Helen M. Roe, 'Tales, Customs and Beliefs from Co. Laois' in *Béaloideas*, Published by Folklore Society of Ireland, Iml.9, Uimh.1 (June 1939)

COLLECTIONS

Journals of the Laois Heritage Society and the journal *Ossory Laois and Leinster*

National Folklore Collection, UCD, manuscripts 36.95.127

National Folklore Schools Collection 1937-1938

WEBSITES

www.facebook.com/laois.archaeology

https://www.facebook.com/laois.heritage.forum

www.facebook.com/pages/Rock-of-Dunamase/1591001321116099

www.laois.ie/heritage

ABOUT
THE AUTHOR

Nuala has had an eclectic career as an actor, storyteller, sometime folklore collector, and Independent Radio Producer.

She trained as an actor with the Abbey Theatre, and was a member of the Abbey Company for five years. She was involved in Theatre in Education and founded TEAM, a touring company for schools. She played the part of Máire, in the first Field Day production of Brian Friel's great play *Translations* in Derry in 1980 and recently she played the title role in *Dear Frankie* by Niamh Gleeson.

Her interest in oral storytelling began in the early 1990s when she founded Two Chairs Company with musician Ellen Cranitch to explore stories with music. She was artist in residence in County Laois in 2002 where she collected and recorded many of local stories, which resulted in a radio series and film, entitled *Tales at the Crossroads*.

She has been involved in story recording projects in the Midlands and also on Cape Clear Island, off the West Cork coast. She has organised and curated many storytelling gatherings and festivals including Scéalta Shamhna, the first Dublin Storytelling Festival and the Farmleigh Festival of Story and Song. Nuala enjoys collaborating with musicians and artists, including the harper and composer Anne Marie O'Farrell, the clarinettist Paul Roe, and the visual artist Rita Duffy.

She lives beside the River Liffey in Dublin. She had two sons, five gorgeous grandchildren and a *slua* of much-loved nieces and nephews.

About
the Illustrator

Rita Duffy was born in Belfast. She received a BA at the Art & Design Centre and a MA in Fine Art at the University of Ulster. She is one of Northern Ireland's ground-breaking artists who began her work concentrating primarily on the figurative/narrative tradition.

Her art is often autobiographical, including themes and images of Irish identity, history and politics. Duffy's work has grown and evolved but remains intensely personal with overtones of the surreal. Homage is paid to the language of magic realism and always there is exquisite crafting of materials. She has initiated several major collaborative art projects and was made an Honorary Member of the Royal Society of Architects, for her developmental work within the built environment. She is an associate at the Goldsmiths College, London and collaborated on an artistic exchange with Argentina and Northern Ireland, looking at the role art has in post-conflict societies. Over the past twenty years she has generated numerous socially engaged projects and designed a series of permanent and temporary public art projects in a wide range of locations and settings throughout Ireland, Britain and beyond.

Firmly committed to her studio based work, her practice now extends to include sculpture and installation work as well as collaborations with architects, poets, filmmakers and a long time collaborator Nuala Hayes.